Marshall
"Major"
Taylor

Marshall "Major" Taylor

WORLD CHAMPION BICYCLIST, 1899-1901

Marlene Targ Brill

Twenty-First Century Books/Minneapolis

Acknowledgments: Many people helped me gather information for this book. Special thanks go to Kisha Tandy, Indiana State Museum; Lynne Tolman, Major Taylor Association; Wilma Gibbs, Indiana Historical Society; Dan Casin, National Sporting Goods Association; Anna Kung, Worcester Public Library; and Barry Parsons, *Worcester Telegram & Gazette*.

Note to readers: To preserve the authenticity of Marshall Taylor's material, the publisher has reprinted certain passages with original racial vocabulary intact.

Twenty-First Century Books
A division of Lerner Publishing Group, Inc.
241 First Avenue North
Minneapolis, MN 55401 U.S.A.

Website address: www.lernerbooks.com

Library of Congress Cataloging-in-Publication Data

Brill, Marlene Targ.
    Marshall Major Taylor : world champion bicyclist, 1899–1901 / by
    Marlene Targ Brill.
       p.   cm. — (Trailblazer biographies)
    Includes bibliographical references and index.
    ISBN-13: 978–0–8225–6610–6 (lib. bdg. : alk. paper)
    ISBN-10: 0–8225–6610–9 (lib. bdg. : alk. paper)
    1. Taylor, Major, 1878–1932—Juvenile literature. 2. Cyclists—
Biography—Juvenile literature. 3. African American cyclists—
Biography—Juvenile literature. I. Title. II. Trailblazer biography
GV1051.T3B75 2008
796.6'2092—dc22   2006003883

Manufactured in the United States of America
1 2 3 4 5 6 – JR – 13 12 11 10 09 08

CONTENTS

Author's Note

Bicycle racing was once the most popular sport in the world. At the turn of the twentieth century, bicycle races attracted more fans than baseball, boxing, and horse racing combined. Six-day, long-distance, and short sprint races offered heart-stopping contests that challenged riders to awesome acts of speed and endurance. Imagine the thrill of soccer's World Cup, the Olympics, or a rock concert. That's the kind of excitement bicycle racing ignited during the late nineteenth century.

Racing champions were the sport's superstars. Professional racers traveled from city to city on riding tours, where they drew huge crowds with their fearless, fast-paced riding. Children collected pictures of cyclists on trading cards the way many collect cards of modern sports heroes now. Race winners received much of the same fame and fortune awarded to top athletes today.

The biggest bicycle star anywhere was Marshall "Major" Taylor. Taylor won his first race when he was just thirteen. From the late 1890s to the early 1900s, he ruled racing as the fastest rider in the world. He won top races, broke speed records, and bicycled to fame on three continents. Taylor's presence added energy to a sport that already claimed the hearts of rich and poor of all ages.

Looking back, Taylor's achievements were even more remarkable considering he was black. He raced during a time when African Americans faced terrible prejudice in the United States. Whites and blacks rarely mixed, and professional bicycle racing was a whites-only business. Any black who dared race—and win—encountered constant attacks.

Yet Taylor remained focused on winning. He held his head high, meeting hostility with courage and amazing skill. His weapon against those who wronged him was not to fight or use dirty tricks, as his rivals practiced. Instead, he beat them fairly.

Taylor became the first black international cycling star. He was the second African American world champion in any sport—boxer George Dixon was the first. Taylor won his races fifty years before Jackie Robinson broke Major League Baseball's color barrier. Taylor represented black Americans in many countries around the world. Throughout his travels, his bravery and sense of fairness shone as a light of hope during a dark era of race relations.

Because of his skin color, history books largely ignored Taylor. Little is known about his life outside bicycle arenas. I pieced together facts I gathered from readings, travels, and interviews to track his life. Here is the story of this incredibly courageous person and champion bicyclist.

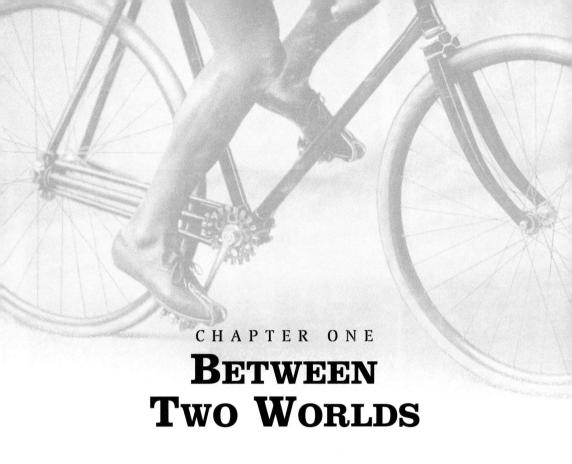

CHAPTER ONE

BETWEEN TWO WORLDS

Marshall Walter Taylor's story began with his birth on November 26, 1878. He was born on a small farm at the western edge of Indianapolis, the capital of Indiana. The two-room, one-story frame house overflowed with ten people—his parents, Gilbert and Saphronia, and his five sisters and two brothers.

Marshall's parents had moved from Kentucky before his birth. Although his parents were free, his grandparents had been slaves in Kentucky before the Civil War (1861–1865). Marshall's father fought with the North in an all-black army company. During the war, they fought to help free slaves everywhere.

But winning a war against slavery didn't change everyone's mind. Postwar feelings against equality for African Americans ran high in many parts of the country. This was certainly true in Kentucky. After Gilbert and Saphronia married, they headed for Indiana, a state where blacks had never been slaves, to raise their growing family.

The Taylors struggled in Indiana. They settled in Bucktown, a poor area mostly inhabited by black people. Marshall's father thought he could find work more easily in Indianapolis, a city exploding with new businesses. Nearby, a large packinghouse prepared hogs for meat, and the railroad carried meat, wheat, corn, and oats across the country. But most skilled and factory jobs were closed to African Americans. Gilbert took odd jobs to support his family. As each child reached working age, each pitched in with chores and paying jobs.

Little Marshall, one of the younger children, did his part to help. He collected firewood, kept his baby

Indianapolis was a growing city in the 1890s with many nice neighborhoods, such as this one on North Delaware Street.

sister, Gertrude, from trampling the corn plants, and carried the wash. Saphronia smiled when Marshall neatly piled firewood higher than his head and carried the entire bundle of wash into the house. He always tried to carry the most, she noticed. He seemed more determined than the other children.

When Marshall was eight, his father took a job as coachman for the Southards, a wealthy white family. Marshall sometimes accompanied his father to work. His job was to walk the horses around the grounds for exercise.

Marshall thought going to the Southards' home was like stepping into a fancy picture. The Southard family lived on a grand estate in a newer, wealthy area of town. The stable for their horses was bigger than Marshall's entire house. Inside the Southard home, there were rooms furnished with chairs and sofas covered in velvet and other expensive materials. Gold-framed pictures hung on walls. The Southards' son, Daniel, seemed to own every toy in the world, including a bicycle. Marshall had never seen so many things in one place.

Since Daniel was the same age as Marshall, the two often played together. Unlike many whites who worried about mixing socially with blacks, Dan's parents encouraged the two boys to be friends. They must have seen something special in Marshall. He was smart. He was polite. He came from a churchgoing family. The Southards thought he was perfect company for their only child. So they asked Marshall's parents if he could live with the family and be Dan's playmate and companion. The Taylors agreed.

Mostly the Southards raised Marshall as if he were their own son. Usually servants and hired help ate in the kitchen. Marshall could go anywhere in the house, and he ate with the family in the dining room. Dan's parents bought Marshall new clothes, including shoes to cover his bare feet. They even dressed the two boys alike.

"He wasn't living around the stables," his daughter Sydney Taylor Brown recalled. "He was reared like their child, and the Southard boy had a tutor. He didn't go to public school. *He* sat *there*, and *my Daddy* sat *here*, and the tutor taught them."

Marshall went everywhere with Dan. Dan's playmates from other rich families accepted Marshall as one of them. He smacked baseballs and tennis balls

This illustration from *Harper's Weekly* shows American boys playing baseball at about the same time Marshall was growing up.

hard. He ran fast, roller-skated fast, and drove a football through the other team's lines. Marshall played some of these games for the first time. He proved to be a fine athlete who matched his friends' skills in every activity.

Shortly after arriving at the Southards', Marshall learned to ride Daniel's bicycle. Bicycle madness had gripped the city. All the neighborhood kids owned the latest model, called a safety. Manufacturers made safety bicycles with two rubber wheels of the same size. They were easier to ride than earlier "ordinary"

Riders had to run and jump onto these early model bicycles called ordinaries. Ordinaries were difficult to ride and expensive.

models with a giant front wheel and small back wheel. Safety bicycles were lighter too.

Not everyone could afford any bicycle, though. At the time Marshall learned to ride, bicycles cost between $100 and $150. That sum was about four months' pay for most factory workers. Marshall's family didn't have that kind of money, especially for a bicycle. Daniel's parents bought Marshall a bicycle like their son's. Thanks to Dan's parents, Marshall was able to learn bicycle tricks and ride around town with the other boys.

For four years, Marshall moved between two worlds. At the Southards', he lived the life of a wealthy child. He wore fine clothes and used fancy linen napkins at meals. He learned to read and write from a tutor. Marshall absorbed the advantages around him like a sponge. He grew sure of himself and his ability to compete equally with friends like Dan. He learned to feel comfortable around white people.

When Marshall visited home, however, he was thrust back into the life of a poor farm boy. Life was different with his biological family—the food, the run-down surroundings, the way everyone talked. Many children might have disliked being away from their parents and brothers and sisters. Not Marshall. He delighted in his expanded world at the Southards'. He was growing away from his family and their values.

Often Marshall felt confused by the different messages he received. His parents, with family roots in slavery, taught him to be careful in what he said to whites.

THE BIRTH OF BICYCLE RACING IN AMERICA

Until 1878, all manufactured bicycles came from England or France. They were heavy, difficult to pedal, and didn't have brakes or gears. The French called their earliest wooden models boneshakers because of how the iron wheels rattled the rider's body.

This early nineteenth-century French bicycle is made of wood.

In 1870 England introduced a high-wheeler known as the ordinary, which reached the top of a man's head. The designer was James Starley. He named his invention the penny farthing because he thought the bicycle's giant sixty-inch-across front wheel "looked like a British penny in relation to tiny rear wheel, the 'farthing [a smaller coin].' " Both wheels were attached to a steel frame instead of a wooden one.

The seat was chest-high, and it required coordination to mount it. A rider had to run alongside the bicycle with one foot on a pedal. When the bicycle gathered enough speed, the rider swung the other leg over the tall frame and leaped onto the seat. Many riders broke bones trying to jump into the high saddle. If the front wheel hit a rock or hole or stopped too quickly, the bicycle flung the rider forward head first. "Taking a header" became a common term to describe the accident.

American reporter Mark Twain wrote about riding an ordinary in an article called "Taming the Cycle." It began: "The bicycle had what is called the 'wabbles,' and had them very badly. In order to keep my position, a good many things were required of me, and in every instance the thing required was against nature."

Bicycles received their first major showing in the United States in 1876 at the Philadelphia Centennial Exposition. To celebrate the country's one-hundredth birthday, the fair displayed the latest inventions. Visitors marveled at the first electric lights, calculator, telephone, and typewriter. One Boston businessman, Albert Pope, particularly liked the ordinary bicycle. He saw bicycles as the transportation wave of the future. Within a year, he arranged to import ordinaries from England.

Pope found it difficult to keep up with sales of ordinaries. Bicycles for sport and transportation were catching on with lightning speed. Bicyclists formed clubs to ride at fairgrounds, on dirt roads, and at outdoor roller skating rinks. To meet demand, Pope decided to build his own bicycles.

In 1878 the first seventy-pound ordinary, called the Columbia, rolled out of the factory. Like boneshakers, these ordinaries bounced and bumped along the potholed, soggy roads of the day. Riders didn't seem to care. They cycled in packs down parade routes on holidays, battling carriages, trolleys, and scared horses for space. The new U.S.-made model marked the birth of bicycling on a large scale in the United States.

On May 24, 1878, another major event in U.S. cycling history took place. That day the first bicycle race took place in Boston's Beacon Park. C.A. Parker of Harvard University beat opponents on ordinaries by pedaling three miles in twelve minutes and twenty-seven seconds. Boston became the U.S. bicycle capital with the first cycling club, the Boston Bicycling Club, and first cycling newspaper, *Bicycling World*. Bicycle racing fever had begun.

At that time, it was often not safe to speak up to a white person. Yet the Southards encouraged him to speak his mind. The Taylors focused on one day at a time, trying to earn enough to feed and clothe a large family. But the comforts Marshall experienced at the Southards allowed him to dream. Life at the Southards taught Marshall he had choices. His future seemed unlimited.

Marshall tried to fit into both worlds, but he really belonged in neither. His daughter later remembered how her dad felt like an outsider at his parents' home. "He was the one sibling in the group the other children didn't care for because he was different from them. You see, they were farm kids. He had all these manners, fine clothes, and the speech. He liked to eat well. . . . So when he came home, he never was popular with his brothers and sisters."

Marshall learned the hard way that not all whites accepted blacks as the Southards did. One day the boys wanted to play at the YMCA. The YMCA offered sports and a place to exercise. YMCAs claimed to be open to all races and religions. But the Indianapolis YMCA was for whites only. Blacks were never permitted on the gym floor, even with white friends who were members.

Dan's friends complained to their parents. No matter how important the adults were in the community, however, they couldn't change the gym's rules. Marshall could only watch from the upstairs gallery of the YMCA while his white friends exercised.

Marshall wrote in his autobiography, "How my poor little heart would ache to think that I was denied an opportunity to exercise and develop my muscles in the same manner as they, and for really no reason that I was responsible for. However, I made the best of matters knowing that I could beat them."

Marshall determined to work harder than those who were prejudiced against him. And he decided he would do everything to beat them in competitions.

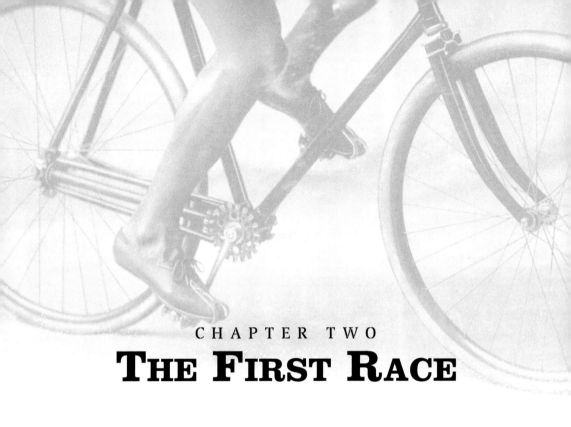

CHAPTER TWO

THE FIRST RACE

At the age of twelve, Marshall's life suddenly
changed. The Southards moved to Chicago, Illinois,
and Marshall's mother wanted him to stay behind.
He was forced to give up his friends, activities, and
comfortable home. He lost everything he had known
for the past four years. Marshall's world fell apart.
"My mother could not bear the idea of parting with
me," he wrote later, "so I dropped from the happy
life of a 'millionaire kid' to that of a common errand
boy, all within a few weeks."

Marshall said good-bye to Daniel with a heavy heart.
He would miss the one boy who knew him better than
his own brothers. He worried about how he would fit
into his family. He feared he would never feel at home
on the farm the way he had at the Southards'.

Slowly, Marshall slipped into the Taylor family routine. Few Indiana schools accepted black children beyond elementary grades. Instead of going to school, Marshall filled his first days at home hauling water from the well, picking vegetables, and looking for a job. On Sundays, Marshall's mother made sure the family attended church together at the African Baptist Church on Michigan Street. After church they often feasted on stewed chicken and white cornmeal hoecakes and always settled in for Bible reading.

As an adult, Marshall said and wrote little about this time in his life. He never mentioned the Southards again. Perhaps it was too painful to recall their leaving and his return to the farm.

Marshall took comfort in the bicycle the Southards let him keep. Many days he escaped for rides. He followed dirt roads along the peaceful White River, past the factories and slaughterhouse. Despite the nasty smells of dead animals and factory waste, Marshall loved the freedom of riding a bicycle. He enjoyed the wind in his face and the way the bicycle responded to his slightest moves. Most of all, the bicycle reminded him of his former playmates and the life he once had.

Having a bicycle enabled Marshall to find a good job. Since few children owned bicycles in his neighborhood, Marshall easily found work delivering newspapers. He liked that he had an excuse to bicycle each day and to keep up his riding skills. A paper route required speed to finish on time. Throwing newspapers from a bag while in motion took coordination.

Not long after returning home, Marshall realized that the bicycle might be his ticket off the farm. Trick riding was gaining in popularity throughout Indiana and around the country. He could perform at fairs, in parades, or before the new bicycle races. After delivering papers, Marshall practiced the riding stunts he learned with his friends. He also invented many new ones. He balanced on handlebars. He twisted and turned and reared up on his back wheel. For the next year, he practiced regularly until he became an expert at jumps, turns, and spins on the bicycle.

Trick riding was popular in the late nineteenth and early twentieth centuries. Marshall spent many hours practicing tricks, such as the one shown here.

One day Marshall needed his bicycle repaired. He rode to the Hay & Willits bicycle store on West Washington Street. After Tom Hay fixed the problem, Marshall leaped onto his bicycle to leave. Tom Hay's jaw dropped as he watched Marshall perform one of the fanciest mounts he had ever seen.

"He asked me who taught me that trick, and when I replied myself he smiled doubtfully," Marshall wrote. "I told Mr. Hay that that was one of my easiest tricks and that I had a number of others that I would like to show him if he was interested."

Hay asked his customers to stand back and challenged Marshall to show him more stunts. Barely breaking a sweat, Marshall dazzled everyone with a selection of spins and mounts. Hay then invited Marshall to perform his tricks outside the store. The boy seemed puzzled by the request, but he followed Hay outdoors.

Again, Marshall performed the tricks and added a few more that used the larger space. Soon a crowd gathered around Marshall, eventually blocking traffic. The police arrived a short time later to see what was causing the backup of horse-drawn wagons. The crowd delighted Hay. If Marshall could attract this many passersby every day, maybe some of them would come into Hay & Willits and buy bicycles. Hay offered Marshall a job if he would perform his tricks outside the store each day.

Marshall later wrote, "I told him I was peddling a paper route and earning $5 a week at it, and that, of course, I would expect a little more for my services, if my mother would allow me to work for him. My eyes nearly popped out of my head when he said, 'I will give you that $35 bicycle, and $6 a week if you will come to work for me.'"

Marshall rushed from the shop to ask his mother for permission. As he hurried along, his mind raced with excitement at the thought of getting paid so much to ride a bicycle, and a new one at that. He burst through the door, breathing hard from the long ride. The story about Hay and the new job tumbled out of his mouth. Seeing Marshall so excited filled Saphronia with joy. How could she say no to him?

A few days later, Marshall headed to Hay & Willits for his first taste of the bicycle business. From then on, he spent each morning sweeping floors, arranging shelves, and dusting bicycle parts. Before four in the afternoon, Marshall changed into a crisp military uniform. The costume glistened with shiny buttons and shoulder braiding. It included a tight-fitting cap. Once dressed, Marshall mounted his new bicycle and amazed passersby with his bicycle stunts. Just as Hay figured, Marshall increased business. Meanwhile, the costume that the straight-backed, serious youth wore gained Marshall the nickname Major. The name stuck.

Another new promotion from Hay & Willits was its first ten-mile road race. The owners hoped that amateur riders would battle bumpy gravel roads and one another for the thrill of winning a gold medal. Future customers would come to watch them.

Hay hung the medal in the window as part of a display to attract entries. Major couldn't keep his eyes off it. After a few days eyeing the medal, he touched it. He held it. One day he gathered his nerve and pinned it to his jacket. He studied himself in the mirror, imagining what it would be like to win a prize for riding a bicycle. "It seemed to me like that would probably be the only chance that I would have to be near such a valuable prize," he wrote, looking back.

But Hay thought differently. The day of the race, Major stood near the starting line to watch one hundred of Indiana's top amateur riders. Bands played and vendors sold ice cream. Since it was Memorial Day, red, white, and blue banners trimmed homes and storefronts.

Hay noticed Major among the thousands of other onlookers lining the roadway. He imagined the sensation this youngster would cause if he raced. He grabbed Major and ordered him to the starting line.

A wave of terror ran through Major's body. These were grown men in the race, and he had never raced. In fact, he had never even seen a bicycle race before! He felt trapped. Hay was his boss, and Major was taught to always mind his elders. Slowly, he mounted the bicycle. As the band began another bouncy tune, tears rolled down his cheeks.

Major remembered, "When Mr. Hay saw that he started to lift me from my wheel, but stopped and whispered in my ear, 'I know you can't go the full distance, but just ride up the road a little way, it will please the crowd, and you can come back as soon as you get tired.' "

Just then Major heard a loud bang from the starting pistol. Hay pushed the shaking, teary-eyed boy into the thick of clanking bicycles. Major scrambled for a place in line. Out of fear, he pedaled—fast.

The crowd roared. Major heard some people laughing at him. But other riders tried to lift the boy's spirits with words of support. After a few miles, Major's legs began to tire. His back ached. His knees hurt. But he was stubborn. Being told he couldn't do something only made him work harder, so he struggled to keep pedaling. "Those words telling me that I could turn back after a short distance inspired me on when it seemed like fatigue was about to overtake me. They made me all the more determined to show my employer that I could go the distance no matter how long it took."

Some distance farther, Major saw a group of riders cycling toward him from the opposite direction. Hay was with them, and he told the cyclists to ride alongside Major. As they rode together, Hay dangled the gold medal for Major to see. He told the boy that he had already ridden half the distance, and he was one mile ahead of his nearest challenger.

Hearing about a chance to win the gold medal revived Major's energy. His mind forced his legs to keep working, even as they begged to quit. Sweat covered his body, and his eyes blurred from weariness. He panted to catch his breath, but he kept pedaling, riding his heart out. To everyone's surprise,

Major crossed the finish line in first place. He was six seconds ahead of the scratch man, the term for the strongest favorite rider.

"Once across the finishing line I collapsed and fell in a heap in the roadway," Marshall wrote. "The first thing I saw on regaining consciousness was that big gold medal pinned on my chest. I had been through a nerve-racking, heart-breaking race, my legs pained me terribly, but I felt amply repaid for my efforts as I scanned that medal. Fast as I had ridden that race I rode with greater speed to my home. My mother laughed and cried in turn as I related the incident of my first race . . . as I was but thirteen years old at the time."

CHAPTER THREE

LEAVING HOME
FOR GOOD

From that first race on, Major's world revolved around bicycles and racing. He worked at the bicycle store every day. After hours he found more races to enter. Some were as far away as Chicago, Peoria, and Springfield, Illinois, each a major Midwest bicycling center. Mostly Major appeared in races for boys under sixteen. Some he won. Other times he took pride in the fact that he held his own. He loved the practice and being around bicycle people.

New developments were improving bicycles. "I clearly recall seeing [racer] William Laurie . . . with the first [air-filled] tires ever ridden on a bicycle race in this country," Major remembered from a Peoria, Illinois, race. Pneumatic, or air-filled, tires were

This is the first bicycle to have pneumatic tires. John Boyd Dunlop created the tires in 1887 for his son, who is pictured above.

lighter than the solid rubber tires used on most safety bicycles. "They revolutionized bicycle racing and the manufacture of bicycles."

Major's parents questioned the hours he spent on the road. They feared he was wasting his time on bicycle pipe dreams. His mother worried about the rough types of people he met. But Major stubbornly refused to give up bicycle racing. At Hay & Willits, he was learning the basics of bicycles and bicycling, and he was meeting bicycle lovers who shared his enthusiasm.

Working at the store was how Major met his next employer, Harry Hearsey, another bicycle dealer. In

A crowd gathers in front of the Hearsey bicycle store in Indianapolis during the early twentieth century. Major worked at a Hearsey store in the late nineteenth century.

the spring of 1893, the fourteen-year-old joined the H. T. Hearsey Company on Pennsylvania Street. The street, which included a larger Hay & Willits store, became known as Bicycle Row.

Working for Hearsey was a step up for Major. Hearsey ran a repair shop, salesroom, and riding school. Major still cleaned and stocked bicycle parts, but his main job was giving bicycle lessons. Even though safety bicycles were easier to ride than earlier models, customers still worried about handling such strange machines. Lessons also brought in new customers, so Hearsey advertised: "Kindly bear in mind that our spacious Riding School, in which our customers may practice free of charge, is provided with padded walls."

Like Hay, Hearsey was a central figure in the Indianapolis riding community. He arranged promotion races and sold the latest safety models. Together Hearsey, Hay, and Willits organized a riding group called the Zig-Zag Club to promote riding. Hearsey allowed Major to participate in Zig-Zag Club riding activities. Club rules restricted blacks from membership, so Major was not allowed to attend social affairs. But he could meet famous racers and learn new bicycling techniques.

By 1893 Major was gaining attention as a crack rider and racer. He had won a few races, and he performed tricks before Zig-Zag Club events. All this attention stirred up feelings against the teenager because of his race. Many white bicyclists felt threatened by a young African American who could outperform and outrace them.

Not all white people opposed Major's riding. Those who valued the sport and anyone with talent championed his racing. Major was fast. His short, tight frame was strong. He was clever at knowing when to stay back and when to pull ahead and win.

One day Major's bicycling friends decided to smuggle him into the one-fifth-mile whites-only Capital City Race Track, even though other white racers might object. The men snuck Major into a dressing room to wait for the right time for him to enter the track. Walter Sanger, a famous rider of the day, had just achieved the speed record for one mile at 2 minutes, 19.4 seconds. After seeing Major practice and race, his friends predicted he could beat that time.

While crowds cheered the announcement of Sanger's winning speed, Major shot onto the wooden track for practice laps. The audience fell silent in disbelief. The judges stared. Major was not on the schedule. Yet here was a black teenager pedaling around the track.

At his friend's signal, the judges started the clock. Major charged ahead as pacers rode in front of him to block the wind that would slow him down. But Major rode too fast, and the pacers couldn't stay ahead of him. By the last lap around the arena, Marshall had pulled ahead. He crossed the tape in 2 minutes, 11.2 seconds. The time was 8.2 seconds under Sanger's record for a mile. It was a new record that lasted the life of the track.

Upon hearing Major's time, the crowd went wild. The cheering brought white riders back onto the track. Once they learned what the fuss was about, they grew angry. Later, in the dressing room, they threatened Major for winning and the track manager for allowing him to race.

That evening Major tackled a one-fifth mile unpaced race to prove his speed wasn't just luck. This unofficial late-night run broke the world record, which had been set in Paris, France, by two-fifths of a second! The records created such hostility that Major was banned from all Indianapolis racetracks.

"I received no pay for my record-breaking mile," Major wrote. "Down in my heart I felt that if I could get an even break I could make good as a sprinter on the bicycle tracks of the country. That was ample pay for me."

One retired high-wheel racing star, Louis "Birdie" Munger, agreed with Major. He believed athletes should be able to develop their talent, no matter what color their skin. Munger, a white businessman who had recently moved from Chicago, remembered seeing Major at races in Indianapolis, Chicago, and Peoria. He thought Major had natural talent on a bicycle.

Munger had met Major at the Hearsey store. He knew that Major lived for bicycling as much as he did. Whenever Munger visited Hearsey, Major plied

Louis Munger *(right)* was a retired racing star who had gone into business. He noticed Major's talent and believed in him.

him with questions and asked to ride his bicycle. Munger liked the young man's enthusiasm for riding, his intelligence, and his good character. After opening the Munger Cycle Manufacturing Company in Indianapolis, Munger hired Major as a housekeeper and company messenger.

Once again, Major moved out of his poor neighborhood, away from his family, and into luxury. He cooked and cleaned at Munger's bachelor home and ran errands between departments at the factory. Major's new life touched every aspect of bicycling. He saw how bicycles were built. He greeted famous cyclists who stayed at Munger's home. Rather than resent his positions as servant and gofer, Major seized the advantages around him, much as he had at the Southards'.

One of the most famous racing stars Major met was Arthur Zimmerman, winner of the first world championship in Chicago in 1893. Zimmerman had just come off his successful 1894 world tour, and he was scheduled to race in Indianapolis. Munger offered Zimmerman a place to stay and sent Taylor to meet his train.

Major's heart beat wildly at the thought of meeting one of his heroes. At the train station, he introduced himself to Zimmerman with a letter from Munger. The charming but shy Zimmerman readily urged the messenger to ride home with him inside the carriage. As they rode, Zimmerman noticed the gold medal around Major's neck. Marshall explained how he won his first medal and many others. Then he shared his dreams of becoming a racer like Zimmerman someday.

Zimmerman seemed to doubt Major's stories. When they reached Munger's house, Zimmerman asked him if Major's stories were true. "Shortly Mr. Munger confirmed all that I had told Mr. Zimmerman about my races and a lot besides," Major recalled. " 'I am going to make a champion out of that boy some day,' said Mr. Munger. At Mr. Zimmerman's request I sat down to the dinner table with them—a great honor indeed."

The two men treated Major as an equal. They told racing stories. And to Major's amazement, Munger shared his plans for the young man with Zimmerman. "I have told Major Taylor that if he refrains from using liquor and cigarettes, and continues to live a clean life, I will make him the fastest bicycle rider in the world."

Before the next day's race, Major had the chance to meet another superstar, Willie Windle. Windle asked about Major's gold medal too. He congratulated Major and shook his hand. Major had shaken hands with two champions, and both men had greeted him as a friend. How unlike the bully amateurs who tried to keep him from racing!

"I was especially impressed with the friendliness of the two of them," he wrote, "especially towards me, a colored boy. I remembered their sterling [fine] qualities and did my best to live up to them, endeavoring to measure up to the high standards of sportsmanship set by them." Major found role models he

Willie Windle *(left)*, a champion rider, was a role model in the bicycling world. Major met him in 1894.

never had until then. For the first time, he had bicycle heroes to follow.

Munger stood by his hopes for Major. He built Major a lightweight bicycle of only fourteen pounds. He rode with Major, guiding his training on roads and tracks. Major responded by working longer and harder. He exercised to improve his speed by chasing steam-engine trains and gasoline-powered motorcycles. He strengthened his legs. He perfected his sprints, the powerful bursts of speed that allowed him to come from behind and cross finish lines first.

News of Major's ban from Indianapolis tracks spread. Luckily, one promoter wasn't scared off. On June 30, 1895, real estate developer George Catterson arranged a seventy-five-mile road race from Indianapolis to Matthews, a town northeast of the city where he had funded new construction. This road event avoided Major's ban from track races.

By this time, bicycling was hugely popular. Major towns built special racing tracks known as velodromes. Thousands of fans attended velodrome and road races. Families dressed in their Sunday best went to watch riders battle one another across the finish line. Bands blared lively patriotic tunes. Racing days turned into giant parties, and bicycle racing made headlines everywhere.

Catterson wanted that kind of attention for his new construction venture. A big race going to his development would let people know it was there. He offered generous prizes to attract the best riders in the state, including Major. But he kept Major's entry a secret, so the other bicyclists would attend.

On the day of the race, the sixteen-year-old hid until the pistol shot signaled riders to push off. After the thirty-six riders sped down the road, he sprang from his hiding place. Major cycled behind the pack for a few miles before several in the race noticed him.

"They made things disagreeable for me by calling me vile names, and trying to put me down, and they even threatened to do me bodily harm if I did not turn back," he wrote. "I decided that if my time had come I might just as well die trying to keep ahead of the

This drawing of Major at sixteen is the earliest known likeness of him.

bunch, so I jumped through the first opening and went out front."

Halfway into the race, the weather changed. Rain poured down in sheets. The heavy drops changed dusty clay roads into mud slides. Riders tired more quickly on the muddy road, which had become almost impossible to travel.

Just six riders made it to the three-quarter mark at the town of Muncie. Out of all the riders to begin in Indianapolis, Major was the only one to reach

Matthews. He crossed the finish line covered in mud, having ridden the last twenty-five miles soaked to the skin.

Catterson pronounced Major "a wonder" and gave him the deed for a house lot in the center of Matthews worth three hundred dollars. Major rushed home to give the deed to his mother. "Of course she was elated over my success," he wrote, "but she made me promise that I would never ride such a long race again."

Attempts to block Major from riding grew stronger after the race. Much of the feeling against him mirrored what was happening all across the country. The more blacks tried to claim rights they gained after the Civil War, the more white communities created hurdles to stop them. Bicycling was the same.

Since 1880 the League of American Wheelmen (LAW) served as the main national bicycling organization. The league set standards for local groups, such as the Zig-Zag Club, and the league campaigned for better roads. At the beginning, the LAW allowed blacks as members, although many local groups in southern states refused to agree to this. In 1894 the Louisville, Kentucky, league convention introduced a rule to deny blacks membership throughout the organization. The only members to vote against the new rule were from the Massachusetts LAW. The rule passed.

With Louisville so close, Munger knew that Major's Midwest opportunities to race were shrinking. At first, he counseled Major to stick with all-black cycling groups. Major joined the See-Saw Circle.

BICYCLE WOMEN

Women riding bicycles? What horrors! What scandal! So said some religious leaders and reporters of the late 1800s. Doctors gave dire warnings about the hazards of women on bicycles. The "weaker sex," doctors claimed, would acquire everything from "heating the blood" to "bicycle face," "bicycle twitch," "bicycle wrists," and "bicycle eye."

But women who dared challenge these notions discovered the freedom of riding bicycles. They cast off their tight corsets, starched ankle-length petticoats, and snug

Full-length skirts, such as the ones these women are wearing *(left),* would often get in the way when riding a bicycle. For this reason, many women started wearing short skirts and bloomers *(opposite page).*

high-heeled boots. They put on looser undergarments, shorter skirts, and lower, more comfortable shoes. Especially brave souls wore large-legged bloomers or other loose-fitting pants. A few even raced. During the 1890s, Tillie Anderson claimed the most medals as U.S. female champion racer.

By 1898 a third of all cyclists were women. Bicycles changed from a "recreational device for wealthy young men to a hobby and mode of transportation for both sexes . . . of modest means." Women's rights leader Susan B. Anthony claimed bicycles did "more to emancipate [free] woman than anything else in the world."

African American riders had formed this group in response to the Zig-Zag Club. Major easily won their competitions throughout the Midwest, even those against top athletes. He craved to compete against the best riders, black or white.

League of American Wheelmen events were popular in the late nineteenth century as shown by this program that includes advertising. Events such as these drew top racers from around the country.

Meanwhile, Munger's fatherly concern for Major brought him trouble. Munger's workers wondered aloud why he bothered with the young man. Businessmen accused Munger of crossing the color line as well as the line between boss and employee to help a young black man. Many questioned why Munger allowed Major to teach cycling to white high school and college youth. They believed he should use white teachers instead.

The resentment came at a time when Munger wanted to expand his business to other towns. Worcester, Massachusetts, offered a growing city with many skilled workers. Worcester was located just seventy-five miles from the bicycle capital in Boston and booming bicycle centers in Springfield, Massachusetts; Hartford, Connecticut, and New York City. These were large markets in which Munger could sell his bicycles.

Munger decided the time was right to move. Knowing Massachusetts was more accepting of all races, he invited Major to join him. Once again, Major said good-bye to his family, this time for good. "Before the train pulled out of Indianapolis," he wrote, "Mr. Munger informed his friends that some day I would return to that city as champion bicycle rider of America."

Major on his bike at the close of the nineteenth century.

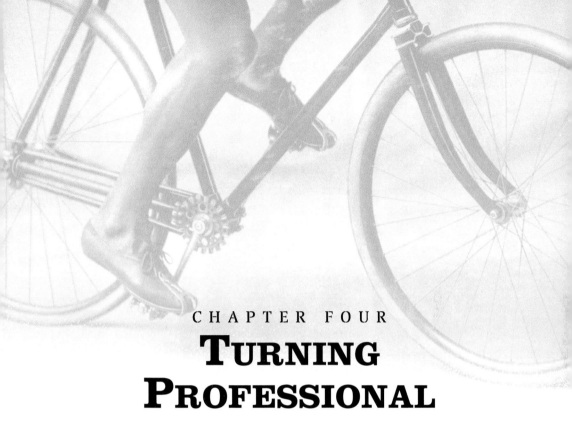

CHAPTER FOUR

TURNING PROFESSIONAL

Worcester turned out to be a good move for both Major Taylor and Munger. Smaller than Indianapolis, the thriving town was home to one hundred thousand people. It boasted a mix of hilly country roads for riding and big-city industry for manufacturing. Town leaders encouraged hard work, creativity, and diversity, which both men embraced. The city's upheld women's rights and housed shredded wheat and monkey wrench factories, all novel items for the day.

With his vast bicycle experience, Munger easily found people to invest money in the Worcester Cycle Manufacturing Company. He set up an office in New York City and opened factories in Worcester and Middletown, Connecticut. Taylor remained Munger's

Major moved to Worcester, Massachusetts, shown here in the early twentieth century, to escape the extreme racism he faced in Indiana.

employee. He no longer lived with him though because Munger had married. Taylor mainly worked as machinist, mechanic, and trusted employee. He delivered products and messages between the two factories and attended bicycle shows with Munger. To earn more money, Taylor took jobs trick riding.

Taylor had learned every aspect of the bicycle business. But he and Munger understood that his true talent was in racing. To race seriously, Taylor needed to get into better shape. As soon as the two settled into their new surroundings, Munger took Taylor to a trainer at the local YMCA. The trainer examined Taylor and found his short legs unusually strong but his upper body weak. The trainer prepared a set of exercises for Major to follow at the YMCA and at home.

Taylor worked on getting in shape with the same focus and determination he applied to riding. Every day he lifted weights and tugged on special pulleys. He swung clubs in patterns around his body to increase upper body strength on his sturdy five-foot seven-inch frame. To boost lung capacity and energy, Taylor performed deep breathing exercises. As always, he rode his bicycle daily.

After a few weeks in Worcester, Taylor realized that bicyclers there weren't prejudiced as they had been in Indianapolis. Here the YMCA had welcomed him. Although city cycling clubs were racially separate, both blacks and whites could enter any race in the region. Major joined the all-black Albion Cycling Club shortly after arriving in Worcester. For a five-dollar membership fee, he found encouragement and a roommate, Benjamin Walker, to share an apartment on Parker Street.

In addition to manufacturing, Worcester also offered countryside with paths for riding.

"When I realized I would have a fair chance to compete . . . I took on a new lease of life," Taylor wrote, "and when I learned that I could join the YMCA in Worcester, I was pleased beyond expression."

Taylor's first race with the Albion Club occurred in October 1895. On a brisk fall day, he took his place for the ten-mile road race. At the sound of the pistol, he charged forward, overtaking a field of sixteen riders. He won with a time of twenty-nine minutes and fifteen seconds. It was a good start in his new home.

The following year, Taylor began his first eastern riding season at a meet in Middletown, Connecticut. The race was sponsored by the local LAW, which would never have allowed him to race in Indiana. Taylor was nervous. This race would show how he measured up against the best amateurs in the area.

A pistol shot signaled the beginning of the race. Taylor stayed behind the other eleven cyclists for most of the trip. As he neared the finish line, he burst ahead, passing each rider in turn. He later wrote, "I won by six lengths and received a wonderful ovation and gold watch which I promptly presented to my friend Mr. Munger in appreciation for some of the many kindnesses he extended to me."

Taylor was living his dream. As he became better known, however, unpleasant things started to happen during races. In one twenty-five-mile road race, Taylor went head-to-head with the lead rider. About a half mile from the finish line, someone threw a bucket of ice water into his face. By the time he regained his bearings, the other rider had crossed the line. Taylor finished in second place.

Not long after that incident, Taylor entered a twenty-five-mile road race at Jamaica, Long Island, in New York. A group of riders plotted to box him in so another rider could pull ahead. But Taylor had become wise to these dirty tricks. "I pretended to be exhausted and made difficult work of holding on to the leaders," he wrote. "The field fell for my stall and immediately dropped their foul tactics. . . . I held my sprint in reserve until we only had a half-mile to go. Then I shot past the bunch and won out by six lengths."

Reporters heralded the new bicycle racing star. Names such as Worcester Whirlwind and Colored Cyclone described his talents. Besides winning races, Taylor was making a name for himself as a trick rider. He performed handstands on the bicycle. He developed a way to pedal backward or to pedal so the bicycle stood still.

At a party at the new Munger Cycle Club, Taylor "rode up a plank eighteen inches wide to the height of six feet, across a platform and down a flight of stairs consisting of fourteen steps, which, considering the amount of room at his disposal . . . was a most ex-traordinary undertaking," wrote one reporter. "Major Taylor is without a doubt, unequalled in this section of the country as a trick rider."

To people in Worcester, however, one of Taylor's greatest feats involved a ride up George Street. The five-hundred-foot downtown stretch between Main and Harvard streets was one of the steepest in Worcester. Local legend claimed that anyone who could climb George Street would become a great racer. Taylor took that as a dare. He not only rode up George Street, he repeated the run fifteen minutes later, the first rider ever to do so.

Within a year, Taylor had either won or placed (came in one of the top three) in all Albion Club racing events. Even though he was still under eighteen years old, other cyclists considered him the top black rider of the United States.

By winter of 1896, Munger had coaxed Taylor into turning professional. As a professional racer, he could enter a planned circuit of races, tour the country and, for the first time, win cash prizes. Professional racing was only three years old. Still, its popularity attracted more than six hundred racers for a hectic season of open road and enclosed arena events. Following the circuit meant living out of suitcases and facing constant pressure to win. But turning professional also could bring fame and fortune—sometimes internationally—as it had for their friend Arthur Zimmerman. Taylor agreed he was ready for the challenge.

Munger pushed Taylor to enter the punishing six-day race at New York City's Madison Square Garden, an indoor arena, for his first professional race. The event made front-page news in most major cities. Win or lose, the bicycling world would surely know about Major Taylor after this race.

Taylor had never ridden on such a small indoor track or taken part in such a long race. His talents were in sprinting, achieving quick bursts of power for short runs. This race required the racers to pedal continuously on a steeply banked wooden track for six days and nights. The only breaks were to eat, sleep, and bathe. Both men knew that if Taylor could conquer this race, he could conquer any event.

The night before the big race, five thousand fans packed Madison Square Garden. Several racers, including Taylor, entered a series of short races designed to whip up enthusiasm for the beginning of the big race next day. "When he first appeared, the

Madison Square Garden was the most famous site of six-day bike races in the early twentieth century.

crowd laughed and chaffed him," wrote one reporter. "Presently, he showed that he could ride fast, and then came the discovery that there was no one in the race who could sprint with him."

Taylor smiled ear to ear as he accepted his first money award for racing. He usually gave his amateur prizes to his mother or Munger. This time, he immediately sent the two hundred dollars to his mother.

At midnight the next night, Taylor waited for the six-day race to begin with fifty of the most experienced long-distance riders. Each rider had a support crew that changed flat tires, cooked food, and fetched drinks. Once the gun fired, however, each rider was on his own. Taylor shot forward, keeping pace behind the front-runner. He tried to follow a schedule of eight hours riding and one hour sleeping. Once rested, he sprinted a few laps to make up the time and pass other riders.

Eighteen hours into the race, Taylor's energy faded. He was hungry, thirsty, and extremely sleepy. To keep Major in the race, his crew tricked him. They told him to ride until the doctor arrived, but they never called one. After three brutal days of riding, they gave him baking soda in water and said it was medicine to keep him awake. Taylor took the bait. Fighting pain, fatigue, and boredom, he survived the next eighteen hours without any sleep.

"It wasn't expected that he would last long in this race," the *Worcester Daily Telegram* reported. "The sprinting he has done ought to have killed him long ago. He jumps out and rushes around with the sprinters as if he hadn't ridden nearly seven hundred miles. . . . His sprints always arouse enthusiasm. When he isn't sprinting he is whistling, and he can whistle as well as he rides." Out of fifteen riders to finish, Major came in eighth place, having logged 1,787 miles and earned his place as a professional racer.

As Major grew older and stronger, he became faster and harder to beat. This photo is from 1903.

CHAPTER FIVE

WORLD CHAMPION

After the six-day race, Munger helped Taylor find a manager, William Brady. Brady arranged the careers of some big-time prizefighters. He knew how to promote his clients, and he wasn't afraid to fight for them. Brady began scheduling Taylor's 1897 season. Meanwhile, Taylor returned to working in Worcester and getting into even better shape.

Taylor led off the next racing season with wins in Philadelphia; Waverly, New Jersey; and Boston. For the first time in his life, he earned a good living. Sometimes, he received up to $850 a day. This was twice what his father made in a year as a coachman. Brady contracted for Taylor to receive an added $1,000 bonus if he broke track speed records. Tayor had already broken records at tracks in Indianapolis and Philadelphia. In those races, however, he had earned no extra payment because he had been an amateur.

As wins piled up, Taylor set his sights on the national championship. But he hit a snag when the LAW racing circuit went south. White southern promoters refused to allow him into their races. Without these races, Taylor could never win enough races to beat other racers in the national standings. Prejudice derailed the season, but Taylor wasn't giving up.

Several promoters allowed Taylor to compete because of widespread public support. Brady understood that the main reason the LAW permitted Taylor to race involved money. The public loved him, and they loved the action-packed races created by his presence. Taylor's appearances meant the races would be exciting—and full. "I have never seen such finishes," a reporter wrote after one race.

Newspapers splashed headlines of Taylor's troubles with white cyclists, which created sympathy for him. The more problems Taylor had with white racers, the more people flocked to see him. Fans booed those who bullied and fouled Taylor and cheered his triumphs against risky odds. Most agreed that if Taylor rode well enough to win, he should be allowed to ride in fair races.

Some riders, however, thought differently. A number of them plotted to keep him from racing and winning. Taylor was used to scrapping for prime riding lanes and to cyclists ganging up and boxing him in. In some meets, riders refused to race against him. Several boycotted (stayed away from) arenas and hotels that contracted with Taylor. A few tried to hurt him to keep him from winning. In one Boston race, a rider drove Taylor off the track. In another an angry rider dragged Taylor from his bicycle and choked him until he passed out. Bruises, scrapes, and threats on his life became routine.

Newspapers carried stories about the bad treatment Taylor experienced. "Taylor now ranks with the fastest men in this country," wrote the *Worcester*

Major Taylor Choked Into Insensibility.

Major Taylor, the plucky Afro-American professional bicycle rider, who won several races at Valley park Saturday, had a thrilling experience at Taunton, Mass., last week Thursday In the mile open race Tom Butler crossed the tape first, with Major Taylor second and W. E. Becker third. Becker was so exasperated at his defeat that he seized Taylor from behind and pulled him from his wheel, choking him into insensibility. The crowd stood up for Major and Becker had a narrow escape from rough handling. Some one ought to have given him a sound thrashing.

This article appeared in the *Cleveland Gazette* on October 2, 1897, after a fellow rider became angry when Taylor beat him. After the race, the rider choked Taylor until he passed out.

Daily Telegram, "but the racing men envious of his success and prejudiced against his color, aim to injure his chances whenever he competes. This conduct robs Taylor of many chances to secure large purses and endangers his life."

Racing judges either ignored fouls against Taylor or issued tiny fines for large offenses. If someone questioned an outcome, most judgments favored the white rider, even if Taylor clearly won. Many judges and reporters blamed Taylor for his troubles, saying he should know his place and not cross the color line.

An angry white passenger orders a black man out of a train car for whites in the 1800s. Taylor often faced racism like this when he raced or traveled to races. This illustration first appeared in the *Illustrated London News* in 1856.

JIM CROW

Restrictions against African Americans had been building since the Civil War. Southern communities passed laws called Jim Crow laws to limit the economic and physical freedoms of former slaves. The name Jim Crow began with Daddy Rice, a white entertainer in the 1830s. Rice blackened his face and sang and danced as a goofy black person named Jim Crow. The character became a popular symbol of black inferiority. Some newspaper cartoons used the character to mock Major Taylor.

By the 1890s, Jim Crow laws prevented African Americans from voting and using the same schools, bathrooms, water fountains, restaurants, and hotels as whites. Blacks had to use separate doors to public buildings, including hospitals, remove their hats to show respect to white people, and move off the sidewalk to let a white person pass. Worst of all, many communities reinforced these senseless laws against African Americans with lynchings and other murders.

The U.S. government refused to pass laws to protect blacks and allow them legal rights. The final blow came from the U.S. Supreme Court in the 1896 *Plessy v. Ferguson* case. Judges ruled that separate railroad cars for blacks and whites did not violate the U.S. Constitution. This decision permitted other laws that separated whites and blacks to remain in effect. African Americans could be legally excluded from a range of everyday activities, including sports. Even worse, the ruling failed to protect blacks who challenged the laws, opening the door to new physical assaults on them. Against this backdrop, Major Taylor began his professional riding career.

Taylor suffered abuse on the road as well. Restaurants refused to feed him. He was denied rooms in hotels where other racers stayed. In Saint Louis, Missouri, no hotel would give him a room, so Taylor found lodging with a black family. To keep his strict training diet, he crossed town three times a day to eat at the railroad station restaurant, the only one that would serve him. "After several meals at this location the restaurant manager very rudely informed me that I would not be welcome henceforth and so instructed the head waiter who was one of my own color," Taylor wrote. "This, however, the waiter refused to do and was promptly discharged for that reason." This treatment forced Taylor to leave town without racing.

Similar insults also forced Taylor to leave Cape Girardeau, a town ten miles south of Saint Louis, without racing. After Taylor left, black supporters pulled their four hundred dollars from the race, lowering purses (prize money) for the remaining racers. This resulted in a contract dispute with the National Circuit Riders (NCR), a new group that ran this and other races. The NCR threatened to cancel Taylor's membership for breaking his contract. Taylor pointed out that he never received the promised housing and that is what broke the contract.

For his part, Taylor never wavered from his desire to win. He always ran a clean race. He was polite and respectful with judges and other riders, no matter how rude they were. "I only ask from them [other riders] the same kind of treatment which I give and am willing to continue to give," he repeated many times. He tried to follow the rules set by the two riding organizations, the LAW and the NCR, even as they masterminded schemes to keep him from reaching his goal of becoming the nation's fastest bicycle rider.

Taylor was a private man, never confiding or complaining to others. To keep up his spirits, he poured every detail of himself into a small pocket diary. "He kept diaries listing every penny he spent," his daughter said. "Twenty cents for headache tablets, 60 cents for laundry, breakfast 25 cents, lodging $2, telegram 25 cents."

Not long after Taylor declared himself a professional, his mother died, on June 10, 1897. It was a terrible loss to him. To honor her memory, he reconnected with his strict Baptist upbringing. He marked the day in his diary, writing simply, "embraced religion Friday, January 14, 1898."

A small Bible accompanied him on his travels. He read passages before each race. Bible quotes peppered many diary entries, providing comfort on especially difficult days. At home in Worcester, Taylor joined the John Street Baptist Church, becoming a respected member of the congregation. He never drank or smoked, as Munger had advised, and he refused to race on Sunday, the Lord's Day, as a promise he had made to his mother.

With renewed hope, Taylor entered his next riding season. He thrilled to accomplish twenty-one first-place finishes and seven world records out of a fifty-race circuit. With the highest national rankings, Taylor clearly stood to win his first national championship. But both professional groups plotted against him. The NCR broke promises not to race on Sunday, which meant Taylor couldn't enter a key race. The LAW suddenly changed the way it counted wins. As in the year before, Taylor was denied the national championship.

Despite the setbacks, Taylor ended the 1898 season winning thousands of dollars and beating the best riders in the country. He broke seven records, riding

Taylor overcame many obstacles in 1898 on his way to becoming one of the best riders in the country and winning thousands of dollars.

the quarter mile in an amazing twenty seconds. He also rode the one-third mile in twenty-seven seconds and the one-half mile in forty seconds. To his fans, Taylor was the national sprint champion, whether other riders acknowledged him or not.

Harry Sager, president of Sager Gear Company, agreed. He offered to pay Taylor to test and exhibit his company's new chainless bicycles during the next season. This invitation made Taylor the first African American to earn money for promoting a

Major was paid to test and exhibit this chainless bike in 1899, making him the first African American to sponsor a product.

product. Taylor began to earn more than ten thousand dollars a year—a huge amount for anyone at the time. He looked toward a brighter future. "If I go out for the records next fall," Taylor told a reporter, "you will see me riding in faster time than ever. I am confident that the maximum speed on the bicycle has not been reached."

The next year, Taylor seized his chance to shine as no black athlete before him had. He arrived in Montreal, Canada, for the world championship in top condition. This was his first venture outside the United States, and fans viewed him eagerly as a favorite for the one-mile world title. More than eighteen thousand supporters filled the stands in Queen's Park as bands blared lively tunes and vendors peddled food and drinks.

Taylor easily won the first two heats, the races that decided who goes onto the finals. Going into the final heat, he knew he had a strong chance of beating finalists from Canada and France. But he worried about the Butler brothers from the United States. Tom Butler was the current U.S. national champion. He and his brother had worked together against Taylor in earlier races.

At the sound of the pistol, the men shot out, keeping a brisk pace. As they crossed the line for the first lap, Taylor saw the other racers were trying to box him in. When the Canadian champ, Angus McLeod, made a break for the finish line, Taylor saw his chance to break out too. He took it.

"Within the sight of the white line, the colored rider crouched lower than ever over his mount and made a finish that would have caused the most sensational of them all to turn green with envy," wrote the *Montreal Gazette*. "Major Taylor fairly lifted himself and his wheel across the line a tire's width ahead of Butler."

Taylor became the first African American to win a world bicycling championship. He rode a victory lap around the track carrying a giant bouquet of roses, beaming at the crowd's wild standing ovation. "I shall never forget the thunderous applause that greeted me," he wrote. "It was the first time that I had triumphed on foreign soil, and I thrilled as I heard the band strike up the 'Star Spangled Banner.'... I never felt so proud to be an American before, and I felt even more American at that moment than I had ever felt in America."

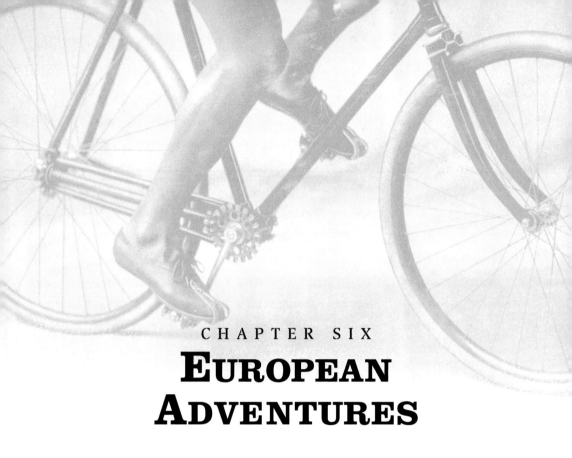

CHAPTER SIX

EUROPEAN ADVENTURES

The glow from the national championship lasted barely a week. During Taylor's next race at Boston's Charles River Park track, the entire field of racers ganged up against him. They surrounded him, closed him into tight pockets, and fouled him repeatedly. Although angry, Taylor never resorted to their dirty tricks or injured his opponents.

Fans booed and shouted their protests on Taylor's behalf, but the judges did nothing. Because Taylor couldn't shake off his enemies, he lost the opening races. "I was a pretty sorely mussed up World's Champion when my rivals had finished with me at the end of the first day's racing," he wrote.

Despite getting banged up, Taylor never lost his nerve or resolve. Once again, being threatened only fueled his desire to win. During the second day's races, Taylor charged to the front of the pack to avoid his attackers. He never looked back—until he had won the half-mile LAW championship. Taylor went on to Peoria to take three first places. Then in Chicago he set a new world record of one minute, nineteen seconds for a paced mile.

Taylor returned to Worcester a hero. Out of twenty-nine events, he took first twenty-two times. Better yet, he had finally won the 1899 national and LAW championships.

Still, the battle against discrimination shadowed him, even to Worcester. At the season's end, Taylor bought a two-story, seven-room house on Hobson Avenue. It was in the fancy new Columbus Park development near Coes Pond. His younger sister Gertrude had been living with him since September and attending Worcester High School. She was gravely ill with tuberculosis, a lung disease, and Major wanted a place to nurse her back to health.

When white neighbors realized a black family had moved in, a group of them protested to the developer. The developer refused to break the deal, so they offered Taylor two thousand dollars more than he had paid to buy back his house. Taylor refused, but not before headlines as far away as Boston expressed support for him and outrage at the community. One newspaper article read: "It was the soil of Massachusetts that was first watered with blood . . . against tyranny and stood

Taylor bought this house on Hobson Avenue in Worcester, Massachusetts, with the money he earned racing.

for equal rights and human liberty. The color line should not be drawn as straight as it appears to be drawn here. Major Taylor is a young man . . . of irreproachable character."

Eventually, the uproar died down, and the Hobson Avenue neighbors accepted their famous black resident. He was quiet, friendly, and gentlemanly, and he was fast becoming one of the wealthiest African Americans in the country.

The Montreal race had thrust Taylor into the highest ranks of cycling celebrities. Requests for him to race poured in from Europe, where bicycling's popularity far exceeded interest in the United States. As he was the best-known U.S. rider in Europe, French promoters saw the world champ as a money-maker. French manager Robert Coquelle offered Taylor ten thousand dollars plus prize money—which could be sizable—to race with the greatest European riders.

Without considering the amount, Taylor turned down the contracts. Many races in Europe took place on Sunday when more people could attend. Taylor refused to bend his no-Sunday rule, even for more money than any athlete had ever been offered. Another reason to refuse was Gertrude, whose health had worsened.

On a different front, the lingering problem of professional cycling membership came up again. The NCR and LAW, which had locked horns over control of racing, came to an agreement. When some members of LAW left and joined the NCR to protest how races were governed, the league agreed to give up authority over professional events.

Taylor felt defeated by this decision. The league had been his safety net, allowing him into professional races without full membership. The NCR, with its strong antiblack core of racers, had barred him from tracks since he left Cape Girardeau. Because of the change, he was put in the awkward position of having to beg those who hated him to reinstate his membership. Otherwise, he faced the end of his racing career. "Little Hope for Major Taylor" screamed the headline of the *Worcester Daily Telegram.*

With threats of more dirty tricks looming, Taylor figured correctly that this was not the time to leave the country. Without a professional organization behind him, he might not be able to compete in 1900. Still, overseas offers planted the idea that one day he could become an international star like his hero Arthur Zimmerman.

Support for Taylor appeared in newspapers and bicycle magazines around the nation. By April the NCR bowed to public opinion and reinstated him as a member. Although he was relieved, Taylor had more pressing problems. Gertrude died a week after he learned about his membership. He had always taken responsibility for his family, and Gertrude's death affected him deeply. He accompanied her body home to Indianapolis and arranged for her burial in Crown Hill Cemetery, where he had buried his mother two years earlier.

So far, 1900 had been a heartrending year. Taylor trained to ease his sadness and to put his troubles behind him. He looked toward another great racing season. More of his races were becoming match races, which pitted two racers against each other. This meant Taylor went head-to-head with the best sprinters around. Each rider put up a certain amount of money, usually five hundred dollars. The winner received the entire purse. Most often, Taylor—or Black Zimmerman, as he was often called—won. One by one, Taylor overtook his rivals. "On the whole Major Taylor is King-Pin among the sprinters," wrote one reporter.

On July 18, 1900, Taylor anxiously prepared for one of his most important events. He was to race at the new saucer-shaped track in Indianapolis named Newby Oval. This was his first race in his native city since Munger took him to Worcester. As Munger had promised when they left, Taylor was returning as world champion. Still, he paced nervously. This was the first race his stern father agreed to attend. The champ wanted to give his father his best show.

For the first half-mile championship race, however, Taylor came in a disappointing second. Upset, he determined to fight harder for the two-mile handicap race. As he was the fastest-rated rider, the rules required Major to start the race behind the other cyclists as a handicap. Being last made little difference to him. Once the pistol shot, he quickly jumped to the front of the pack, flew around the track, and crossed the finish line three lengths ahead of his next opponent.

The elder Taylor congratulated his son but he seemed dissatisfied. From all the newspaper accounts of Taylor as the fastest racer in the world, he had expected his son to beat his rivals by more time. What bothered Gilbert more, though, was seeing his son start in last place with white boys ahead of him. He worried that his son was "being picked on again because of [his] color." Taylor tried to explain about reporters, bicycling, and handicap races. "This was my father's idea how fast his boy could ride a bicycle, and also his idea of what I was up against because of my color," Taylor wrote.

Despite the disappointing encounter with his father, Taylor rode a great 1900 season. He finished with enough victories to top the NCR, totaling twenty points more than his next closest rival. He had accomplished his dream. He had earned the undisputed title of sprint champion of the United States.

Happy and relieved, Taylor decided he needed a break. The twenty-one-year-old thrived on fans and applause. But the constant stress of traveling, racing, and battling racist judges and opponents was taking a toll. His opponents required him to be on high alert through every race. Pushing in front to avoid their assaults created extra strain on his body. And even though Taylor never boasted about his wins, not one rival congratulated him before or after a race. Other riders banded together against him. He always stood alone.

For a change of pace, Taylor used his fame to enter vaudeville, the popular live variety shows of the day. He had natural talents for singing and playing piano and mandolin. Taylor also rode a bicycle on stage, only he balanced his bicycle on a stationary machine with rollers called the home trainer. His act involved pedaling against another rider, Charlie "Mile-a-Minute" Murphy, on their home trainers. Audiences followed their favorite's progress in five-mile heats with arrows connected to counters on the bicycles. Fans loved the act. The cyclists performed at the Worcester Park Theater and throughout Massachusetts with the Keith Vaudeville Company, the oldest and biggest show around.

While touring, Taylor received two proposals. One was a one-thousand-dollar contract to ride Iver Johnson Arms & Cycle Works bicycles for the next

"Mile-a-Minute" Murphy earned his nickname by racing a measured mile in 57.8 seconds behind a single car train in 1899.

two seasons. The other proposal came from Robert Coquelle in France. He offered Taylor three thousand dollars to appear in six midweek matches on European tracks. Taylor would race against the biggest names in Europe—and not on Sundays. Taylor signed both contracts.

He also wrote two life-altering words in his diary on October 11, 1900: Daisy Morris. This was

Daisy Morris met Taylor at a social function in Worcester in the late 1890s.

Taylor's first mention of a woman in his diary. He said that Daisy was special. She was the tall, stately, and educated daughter of a white father and black mother from Hudson, New York. In 1897 she had moved to Worcester to live with her aunt and uncle, the Reverend Louis Taylor, after her mother died. Daisy Morris traveled in the most refined black social circles. These same gatherings probably included the reserved but handsome bicyclist. The two had become engaged by Taylor's sailing date several months later.

Taylor spent the months of early 1901 in a brutal whirlwind tour. He took part in fifty-seven races in sixteen European cities. In Europe Taylor experienced none of the racism that hounded him back home.

LA VIE AU GRAND AIR

ABONNEMENTS
s . . . Un an 14 fr. | ÉDITION DE LUXE
.RTEM¹⁴ — 15 fr. | FRANCE... Un an 30 fr.
NGER. — 20 fr. | ÉTRANGER — 40 fr.

10 Mars 1901. — N° 130
Rédaction et Administration : 370, rue Saint-Honoré, PARIS (1ᵉʳ Arrᵗ).

PUBLICITÉ
PAGES DE COUVERTURE, la ligne.   1 fr
LA PAGE   600
ENCARTAGES   500

Taylor enjoyed great fame in Europe, as well as a break from the constant racism he experienced in the United States. Here he appeared on the cover of a French cycling magazine in 1901.

Europeans treated him as a champ. He stayed at the best hotels and ate at top restaurants. European cyclists accepted him for his talent. Crowds flocked to see the world's best rider.

Taylor showed off his star power wherever he raced. His smooth, controlled style contrasted well with the more energetic European competition. He finished first in forty-two events of various formats. In each country, he bested the national hero.

The highlight of the tour paired Taylor with the 1901 world sprint champ, Edmund Jacquelin, in Paris. Since the 1901 world championship had been on Sunday, Taylor hadn't entered. He was eager to face Jacquelin to keep his reputation as the best sprinter in the world. But Taylor rarely rode well on cold days, and the day of the race turned bitterly cold. Even bundled in a thick sweater, he lost two straight heats against Jacquelin. What Taylor found worse than losing, however, was the way Jacquelin thumbed his nose as he passed the frozen rider.

Two weeks later, the two faced off again. Thirty thousands fans paid top prices to see the two champions compete for $7,500, an amount worth close to $100,000 today. Taylor was determined to erase the insult in their best-of-three series. This time the weather cooperated. At first, the two challengers kept pace, each pedaling his fastest. But Jacquelin's insult burned inside Taylor. As he rounded the last quarter of the run, Taylor bolted away from Jacquelin. To thunderous applause, he crossed the finish line four lengths ahead of the Frenchman.

"I quickly pulled a small, silk American flag from my belt and waved it vigorously in front of the vulgar Jacquelin while we circled the track. This was my greatest triumph in Paris," Taylor wrote later.

Jacquelin's defeat so outraged the proud French track director that he paid Taylor in small coins. A small wheelbarrow was needed to haul them away.

2ᵉ COLLECTION FELIX POTIN

MAJOR TAYLOR

CYCLISME

Taylor appeared on this French trading card, one in a set featur-
ing sports figures from the early twentieth century.

CHAPTER SEVEN

FALLING STAR

Taylor's career reached its peak in Europe. Europeans admired him as a cyclist and praised his hard training, bright smile, and good sportsmanship. Wherever he traveled, fans greeted the champ warmly and showered him with social invitations. His skin color only made him seem more interesting and attractive.

Taylor hoped to stay longer to keep his winning streak going. The NCR, however, refused to release him from upcoming races in the United States. With newspaper reports of his successes broadcast everywhere, Taylor had become a greater drawing card at home. Once again, he faced a loss of professional membership if he broke a racing contract.

At first Taylor considered giving up U.S. races. This would end the vile treatment from U.S. cyclists for good. The problem was the NCR had become a member of the International Cyclists Union. Without NCR membership, Taylor could not ride on any track, European or American. With regret, he said good-bye to his European friends but vowed to return.

One bright spot in coming home was his marriage to Daisy Morris on March 21, 1902. The wedding took place in Ansonia, Connecticut, where her uncle, the Reverend Taylor, led the congregation. The newlyweds took a short honeymoon. Afterward, they moved Daisy's belongings into Taylor's Worcester home. Then the new bride went back to live with her aunt and uncle while Taylor raced a second triumphant European tour. Taylor missed his wife terribly and sent her many postcards from the European cities he wanted her to see.

Upon return to the United States, Taylor faced a new, more dogged rival. Floyd MacFarland, a racist riding champ from San Francisco, organized other bikers to fix the outcome of races and harass Taylor. For some reason, MacFarland angered the normally calm twenty-four-year-old. Perhaps it was the kindnesses Taylor experienced in Europe. Perhaps it was MacFarland's sneering comments when Taylor quoted the Bible. Taylor seriously considered retiring for the first time. The constant backbiting was sapping his joy of racing. On top of that, a fickle public began to embrace a new craze, the automobile.

Floyd MacFarland's racism made Taylor's return to the United States difficult.

Taylor's friend Zimmerman had warned him to go out on top. Taylor had earned thirty-five thousand dollars during the 1902 season, probably the highest salary of any U.S. athlete. He still claimed seven world records and would probably be the world champion, if he would compete on Sundays.

As Taylor considered leaving racing, a cable arrived from Australia. A booking agent offered him five thousand dollars to race in three Australian cities with no Sunday events. The deal interested Taylor. Australia would complete his career, and he could bring Daisy on an expense-paid foreign tour.

Taylor and his wife, Daisy, enjoyed their first years together in Australia.

The Australian tour began two years of charmed living for the Taylors. Beginning in 1903, they traveled the world, making two trips to Australia and three to Europe. Everywhere they went, people welcomed them like royalty, and Taylor raced before adoring crowds.

After the sorry treatment he received from U.S. riders, Taylor often felt overwhelmed by the warmth he encountered in other countries. During his first

Australian trip, he wrote, "I could not restrain my tears as I looked over the side of the liner and saw hundreds of boats...decked out with American flags with their whistles tooting and men and women aboard them with megaphones greeting me with, 'Welcome Major Taylor!'" Australians called their love affair with Taylor and his winning appearances the Major Taylor Carnival. When Daisy gave birth to their daughter in Sydney, the capital of Australia, they named her Rita Sydney, and they called her Sydney.

Taylor *(far left)* lines up for a race in Australia in 1904.

Taylor's second year of racing in Australia featured almost one hundred races, but the tour ended badly. He seemed worn out from his recent European tour. Taylor was able to push his body to take thirty-two first places and twenty-two second places out of his first sixty-five races. But he was tired, and his nasty U.S. rivals, MacFarland and Iver Lawson, appeared in Australia and whipped up feelings against him. This time, Australian riders, tired of losing to Taylor, embraced MacFarland's ruthless plans to block Taylor from the prize money. Some judges joined in, calling bad decisions in favor of opponents. In Melbourne, Lawson fouled Major in one of his worst crashes. The judges suspended Lawson. But Major was so badly hurt, he canceled the rest of the season and set sail for San Francisco.

After an enthusiastic sendoff from Australia, the family encountered cruel color barriers in San Francisco. No hotel or restaurant would serve them. They searched most of the day for food and lodging with their seventeen pieces of luggage. They also had a collection of pets, including a kangaroo, several colorful parrots, and a cockatoo that said, "Major! Major! Hallo Boy!" Their one meal came after a white Australian biker friend bought food while Taylor, Daisy, and infant Sydney waited outside.

Although angry, Taylor bore the slights with his usual grace. "I bear no animosity [ill will] toward the people of that state [California], nor toward Floyd MacFarland a native son . . . or any rider from else-where. . . . As the late Booker T. Washington, the great Negro educator, so beautifully expressed, 'I shall allow no man to narrow my soul and drag me down, by making me hate him.'"

At home in Worcester, the buildup of insults and physical attacks preyed on the exhausted biker. The controlled manner that helped him train and race crumbled. Taylor suffered a nervous breakdown. Under doctor's orders, he canceled his next year's races at home and abroad.

Promoters only seemed concerned about their money. The NCR went after Taylor for not racing with them. Coquelle sued him for breaking his European contract. This time Taylor didn't care. After eight years of constant racing, the twenty-six-year-old needed to rest.

For much of the next three years, Taylor drove around town in the French automobile he brought back from one of his tours. It was one of the only cars in Worcester. He watched Sydney grow, fought his lawsuits, and tried to keep busy. Friends and church activities helped relieve the boredom. Many distinguished black Americans came calling.

"He was a great guy in Worcester," recalls his daughter. Over the years "William E. B. DuBois [writer and educator], Dr. Charles Drew [creator of the blood bank for storing blood plasma], and Jack Johnson [the first black heavyweight boxing champion] were among his visitors."

At the end of 1906, Coquelle offered Taylor a way to erase his debts and end the lawsuits. He wanted Taylor to race in Europe again. Besides a lower fee,

Heavyweight boxing champion Jack Johnson visited Taylor after he returned to the United States in 1904. Johnson was one of many famous black American visitors.

though, Taylor would have to race on Sundays. He was torn. He felt he needed the money to care for his wife and daughter, and he wanted the lawsuit to end. He also believed he had something to prove. He bristled at racist attacks that assumed he or any black was inferior to whites. After much thought, Taylor agreed to the deal, and the Taylor family sailed overseas.

Taylor's return created a big splash in the French press. Stores stocked a book about the champ. A new song, "Le Nègre Volant" (The Flying Black Man), played throughout Paris. Even with all the excitement, everyone expected Taylor to lose after such a long break from racing. At almost thirty, he was old compared with the new crop of young racers, and he looked out of shape and overweight.

Taylor attacked training with his usual zeal. After six weeks of exercise, boxing, and riding, he lost twenty-six pounds and resumed his form. But good form wasn't enough at first. He fell during races. He lost to faster riders. One headline shouted, "Colored Bicycle Rider Abandons Resolution Not to Race on Sunday and Is Beaten."

Taylor made headlines in the press when he returned. Newspapers such as *Le Vélo (The Cycle)*, which the French cyclist above is holding, were devoted entirely to the country's love of cycling.

After a slow start, Taylor regained his speed and confidence. By the end of 1908, he had established one track and two world records. "Taylor astonished the racing world by showing practically the same speed that made him a marvel of the racing game several years ago," a reporter wrote. The 1909 season followed the same pattern. After several losses, Taylor amazed the world with thirty-two first places and thirty second places out of seventy-two races in four months of competing.

Encouraged, Major decided to return for the 1910 season. But by then, he showed his thirty-two years. He entered more races but won fewer. For the first time in his career, none of his tricks worked. He could no longer escape the fact that his career was in decline. He had trouble sleeping. He worried about making enough money.

Without the support of Daisy and Sydney, who had stayed at home, Taylor grew sad and lonely. He poured out his heart in letters to them. "Be sure to pray for me all the time," he begged Daisy in one letter. "You know how I feel that I need your prayers and sympathy just now more than ever before." Seeing his career fall apart, Taylor wrote, "If I fail to win this event and do not show any better form than I have so far this season, I cannot hope to return again next season."

In one last gasp, Taylor finished the tour on top. At his final event in Roanne, France, he won two out of three matches. In the first victory, he bested Victor Dupré, the current world champion. In the second, he beat Gabriel Poulain, another of France's finest riders.

By the end of the 1907 season, Taylor was able to beat the world champion, Victor Dupré *(above)*.

These heats would be Taylor's last races overseas. He returned to the United States circuit the following summer. But the fire had left his jumps and sprints. Finally, the superstar athlete retired for good.

Taylor poses with his wife, Daisy, and daughter, Sydney, in 1907.

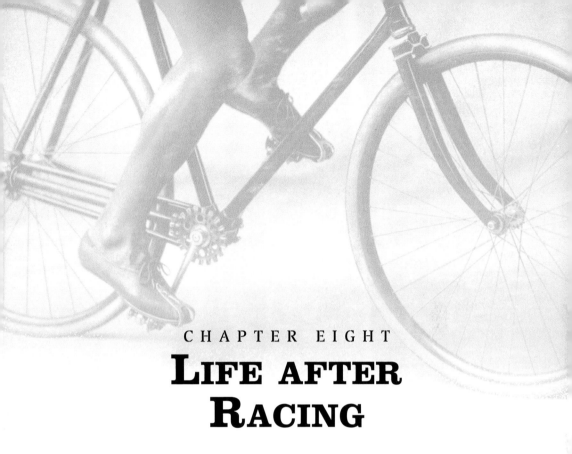

CHAPTER EIGHT
LIFE AFTER RACING

Despite money concerns, bicycle racing had served Taylor well. Always thrifty, he had saved about seventy-five thousand dollars by the time he retired. He was the richest black man in Worcester and one of the richest in the United States. Taylor owned a comfortable home, three apartment buildings, an automobile, a motorcycle, and rooms full of medals, jewelry, and treasures from around the world. These riches gave Taylor some freedom to relax after the taxing riding season. But he still worried about supporting his family and finding a future source of income.

Mechanics and engineering excited Taylor most after cycling. He was a skilled mechanic and inventor already. Bicycle manufacturers made the handlebar extension he designed standard on most bicycles. He decided to take his bicycle skills and use them to build a business in the fast-growing automobile industry.

Taylor applied for entry into Worcester Polytechnic Institute to acquire more training. The school rejected him, supposedly for lack of a high school diploma. He never would have been able to attend high school in Indianapolis. Always determined, Taylor took his savings and invested in what turned into a string of failed businesses. He formed the Excello Oil Manufacturing Company and invented a type of automobile tire. His Major Taylor Manufacturing Company produced the first machines for repairing tires in Massachusetts. When production of these inventions lost money, Taylor opened a tire repair business.

"Father had the idea of using money to make money, but he didn't," Sydney remembered. "The things he involved himself in were things I think he didn't know enough about. He used masses of money to get his projects off the ground. But he involved men who were supposedly his friends, and eventually they got the whole thing away from him."

Other money troubles followed. The tire repair business never turned a profit. Renters refused to pay their rent. Then Taylor's health began to decline. The years of constant training left him with an enlarged heart. In the 1920s, he suffered a bout of shingles, a painful nerve disease, that further damaged his heart and kidneys. He spent long periods of time in and out of the hospital.

Over the years, Taylor gave money to his sisters and brothers. When he needed them, they never returned the help. "In his later years I think he wanted to be nice to his family, but they only saw him as a source of money and they bled him . . . with [their] bills," Sydney recalled. "[They] sent bills and I guess my mother had a hard time persuading him that he had to stop paying them."

Without a steady income and with mounting hospital bills, savings melted away. Taylor was forced to sell the house, and the family moved into a small apartment on 14 Blossom Street. As Taylor's illness dragged on, he sold Daisy's jewelry and other cherished possessions. Finally, Daisy went to work as a seamstress. The move and Daisy's job marked a terrible defeat for the proud champion and a woman accustomed to comfort and elegance.

Taylor occupied himself at home by writing an autobiography. He felt discouraged and depressed. A trip down memory lane reminded him how successful he had been. More important, Taylor believed the story of his life and struggles would inspire other young blacks to strive for success in a racist world.

"About the time I came along, there weren't too many black kids who were even in college," Sydney explained. "Major Taylor wanted young black kids to know that whatever they wanted to do, if they *really* wanted to do it, to get in there and try."

In 1926 Harry Worcester Smith, a friend and noted sports figure of the era, organized an appeal to raise money for Taylor. Smith wrote an article in the *Worcester Evening Gazette* that told of Taylor's misfortune and reminded readers about his fame. "A Champion Laid Low: An Appeal Issued In Behalf of Major Taylor, Veteran Sportsman, Whose Fame Was Worldwide Just a Few Years Ago" read the headline.

The article sounded an alarm around the world. Contributions poured in from Canada and Australia, places where fans remembered the cyclist fondly. In the end, the appeal collected about twelve hundred dollars. Although grateful, Taylor appeared ashamed that he needed the money. In the photograph for Smith's article, he looked smartly dressed in a bowler hat, tie, and tailored overcoat, but he stared past the camera, looking stern, almost embarrassed. The money helped Taylor finish his book, which took several years. It also paid for printing it.

Family relations grew strained under the weight of money problems and Taylor's unbending character. In 1930 Daisy left her husband and moved to New York City. Sydney had already graduated from Sargent School of Physical Culture in Boston and had found a physical education teaching job at West Virginia State University. Neither she nor Daisy ever saw Taylor again. "He was a very controlled man," Sydney remembered. "He was a rigid person. He never had whiskey around—no eggnog at Christmas time—and no card playing, absolutely very rigid. And I think if he hadn't adhered to them so closely he would have enjoyed his life more and my mother would have enjoyed her life more."

Taylor felt abandoned by his wife of twenty-eight years. He could no longer bear living in a city where his life fell apart.

James Bowler, a former cyclist and then Chicago alderman, heard about Taylor's troubles and offered him a job. The same year Daisy left, Taylor filled his car with unsold copies of his autobiography and headed for Chicago. He found a place to live at the South Wabash Avenue YMCA in Chicago's

Moulding Christian Character In Men and Boys
The Wabash Avenue Department

Young Men's Christian Association

Young men coming to Chicago, register, lodge, or find a home in our thoroughly modern, well kept and convenient dormitory. Special rates and cordial welcome to transients.

Men who know, enjoy their meals in our delightful cafeteria. Home-cooked wholesome food is served at minimum prices. Private dining room for parties.

Complete equipment in gymnasium, natatorium, game rooms, lobby, and class rooms, with a trained staff of secretaries and directors always at the service of the membership.

An attractive, scientific program of all-round activity is promoted throughout the year, varying with the seasons but constant in promoting the "More abundant life."

VISIT!   JOIN!   BOOST!
Address: 3753 Wabash Ave., Chicago, Ill.
Telephone: Boulevard 9540

During the last years of his life, Taylor lived at the South Wabash Avenue YMCA in Chicago. This YMCA advertisement is from 1923.

Bronzeville neighborhood. The Y was the hub of Chicago's African American civic and social groups. For the first time since his childhood, Taylor lived in an all-black community.

No records exist of whether or for how long Taylor worked for Bowler. Reports indicate that Taylor continued to sell his books. When few of his neighbors could spare $3.50 for a copy, he called on former cyclists in white neighborhoods. By now Taylor looked much older than his years, yet he always dressed in a business suit and wore glasses. Despite his proud,

Taylor lived and worked in the South Wabash Avenue area of Chicago *(above)* from 1930 to 1932.

formal appearance, Taylor barely made enough money to survive.

By the age of fifty, Taylor's health had worsened. In March 1932, he suffered a heart attack. Bowler helped him get surgery and treatment at Provident Hospital, the best private hospital in the black community. When Taylor's condition declined further, Bowler moved Taylor to Cook County Hospital. He died, at the age of fifty-three, on June 21, 1932, in the hospital's charity ward.

Few people attended Taylor's burial in the poorest section of Mount Glenwood Cemetery, a racially segregated site thirty miles south of downtown Chicago. The African American *Chicago Defender* was the only U.S. newspaper to honor his death with a notice. No stone marked his grave.

In 1948 the Olde Tymers Athletic Club of the South Wabash Avenue YMCA, a newly formed group of former bicycle racing stars, learned the story of Taylor's death. They approached Frank Schwinn, owner of the Schwinn Bicycle Company, to help them restore the memory of the world champion. Schwinn provided a tombstone and paid workers to move Taylor's body to a more respected location in the cemetery.

On May 23, 1948, about one hundred people gathered in the cemetery's Memorial Garden of the Good Shepherd. Ralph Metcalfe, 1936 Olympic gold medalist and congressman, delivered the main address. The cycling club celebrated Taylor's spirit with an engraved bronze tablet for the headstone.

Along with Taylor's image, it read: "Worlds' champion bicycle racer—who came up the hard way—without hatred in his heart—an honest, courageous and God-fearing, clean living gentlemanly athlete, a credit to his race who always gave out his best—gone but not forgotten."

SHARING MAJOR TAYLOR'S STORY

For years Taylor's story remained untold except to a few die-hard bicycle fans. Then Worcester residents formed the Major Taylor Association to remember the Worcester Whirlwind. Articles appeared in Massachusetts papers. Black groups acknowledged him. Taylor became part of the Worcester school teaching curriculum, so boys and girls could learn about their local hero. Each year since 1998, Worcester students have held read-a-thons to help raise money for a Major Taylor memorial statue to stand in front of the city library. In 2006, the Massachusetts legislature approved a bill to add $205,000 to the more than $70,000 already raised to build Taylor's statue.

Indianapolis, too, recognized its native son. In 1984 city leaders named a new bicycle racetrack the

One of Taylor's bicycles, a Peugot, is on display at the U.S. Bicycle Hall of Fame in the ADT Event Center at The Home Depot Center in Carson, California.

Major Taylor Velodrome. The same year, the Chicago Bicycle Federation started work to create the Major Taylor Bike Trail, a scenic six-mile route through the tree-lined Beverly and Morgan Park neighborhoods. These honors came more than one hundred years after Indianapolis barred Taylor from racing in its two velodromes.

Interest in Taylor increased after the release in 1988 of *Major Taylor: The Extraordinary Career of a Champion Bicycle Racer* by Andrew Ritchie. Bicycle groups with his name sprang up in several states, including Illinois, California, Minnesota, Texas, New York, and New Jersey. A 1992 television movie, *Tracks of Glory*, highlighted his racing seasons in Australia.

Other honors followed. In 1996 Taylor's great-granddaughter Karen Brown-Donovan accepted the Korbel Lifetime Achievement Award in Taylor's name from USA Cycling, the bicycle racing governing body. The LAW, which had not enforced its ban on African American membership for years, formally removed the ruling in 1999. Four years later, the Institute for International Sport named Taylor their 2003 Sports Ethics Fellow for his honesty and fair play in athletics and everyday life.

I first learned about Marshall "Major" Taylor while researching a book about Indiana. As I drove through Indianapolis, I noticed the Major Taylor Velodrome. I became curious about the history of velodromes and how this one got its name. I contacted the Major Taylor Association, read Taylor's autobiography, and looked at memorabilia in the Indiana State Museum. I traveled to libraries and historical societies in Indianapolis and Worcester. In each city, I read newspaper articles and personal letters and visited where Taylor had lived and worked. I wanted to tell the story of the champion bicyclist who was the fastest in the world.

TIMELINE

1878   Marshall Walter Taylor is born on November 26 in Indianapolis to Gilbert and Saphronia Kelter Taylor.

1886–1891   Taylor lives with the wealthy white Southard family.

1892   Thomas Hay hires Taylor to perform bicycle stunts in front of his bicycle store, Hay & Willits. Taylor's costume is a military uniform, which earns him the nickname Major.

Hay pushes Marshall to enter his first race, which he wins.

1893   Taylor works for H. T. Hearsey, another Indianapolis bicycle dealer.

Taylor unofficially breaks the speed record for the one-fifth mile.

1894   Taylor takes a job with Louis Munger.

1895   Taylor moves to Worcester, Massachusetts, with Munger.

1896   Taylor unofficially breaks the one-mile paced and unpaced world track records in Indianapolis and is banned from the Capital City track.

Taylor finishes eighth in his first professional race, a six-day continuous event at Madison Square Garden in New York City.

1897   Marshall's mother, Saphronia, dies.

1898   Taylor earns seven world records, including riding the quarter mile in twenty seconds.

1899   Taylor wins the one-mile world championship in Montreal, Canada.

Taylor sets a new world record for the one-mile race, with one minute, nineteen seconds.

1900   Taylor becomes the recognized U.S. sprint champion.

Taylor's sister Gertrude dies.

Taylor takes a short break from racing and performs in vaudeville theater.

1901   Taylor competes in his first European tour, beating each national champion.

1902	Daisy Morris and Marshall Taylor marry on March 21 in Ansonia, Connecticut.
1903–1904	Taylor races in Australia, Europe, and New Zealand, with brief rest stops in Worcester.
1904	Taylor suffers a nervous breakdown and cancels tours for almost three years.
1907–1910	Taylor makes a comeback that lasts for three seasons. By the third season, his career is in serious trouble.
1910	Taylor retires from racing for good at the age of thirty-two.
1910–1925	Taylor invents a type of automobile tire. He enters a series of unsuccessful businesses. His health begins to decline. Taylor begins writing his autobiography.
1930	Daisy leaves Taylor. Taylor moves to Chicago to sell his self-published autobiography.
1932	Taylor dies on June 21 at the age of fifty-three in the charity ward of a Chicago hospital and is buried in an unmarked grave.
1948	Former professional bicycle racers receive money from Frank Schwinn, owner of Schwinn Bicycle Company, to rebury Taylor with a headstone in a more respected section of the cemetery.
1984	Indianapolis names its new bicycle racing track the Major Taylor Velodrome.
1992	The made-for-television movie *Tracks of Glory* highlights Taylor's Australian tours.

BICYCLE TALK

crack rider: a leading bicycle rider

handicap race: races in which slower riders are given a time or distance advantage. Those judged fastest, or scratch riders, start last and must ride harder, longer, and faster to win.

heats: a series of races that decide who advances to the final race

home trainer: a machine with rollers that allows bicyclists to pedal their bicycles without moving

lap: one turn around a track

match race: a race between two riders; the final race in a series of races that pits two riders against each other

ordinary: a type of bicycle common in the nineteenth century that has one sixty-inch front wheel and a smaller back wheel; also called a high wheel

pacing: when one rider cycles in front of another rider to cut down on the wind, so the rider in the back gains speed without the force of wind slowing the ride

pneumatic tires: air-filled tires

pocketing: when riders work together to restrict free movements of one rider on the road or bicycle track

safety: the first type of bicycle to have two wheels of equal size. A chain connects the pedals to the rear wheel, much like modern bicycles

scratch man: the strongest and fastest-rated rider

sprint: quick bursts of speed, usually applied in short races of less than five miles or for final laps

velodrome: an arena for bicycle racing

SOURCES FOR QUOTATIONS

11   Andrew Ritchie, *Major Taylor: The Extraordinary Career of a Champion Bicycle Racer* (Mill Valley, CA: Bicycle Books, 1988), 15.

14   David Chauner and Michael Halstead, *The Tour De France Complete Book of Cycling* (New York Villard, 1990), 2.

15   Jay Pridmore and Jim Hurd, *The American Bicycle* (Osceola, WI: Motorbooks, 1995), 32.

16   Ritchie, 15–16.

16–17   Marshall Major Taylor, *The Fastest Bicycle Rider in the World* (Brattleboro, VT: Stephen Greene Press, 1928), 1.

18   Ibid., 1–2.

21   Ibid., 2.

21–22   Ibid.

23   Ibid., 2–3.

23–24   Ibid., 3.

24   Ibid.

25   Ibid., 4.

26   Ibid., 5.

27   Ritchie, 24.

30–31   Taylor, 7.

33   Ibid., 13.

33   Ibid., 12.

33   Ibid., 9.

35–36   Ibid.

41   Ibid., 13.

46   Ibid., 14.

46   Ibid., 16.

47   Ibid., 17.

47   Unidentified article in Taylor's personal scrapbook at the Indiania State Museum, probably from the *Worcester Daily Telegram*, January 1896.

49–50   "Taylor Riding in Fifth Place," *Worcester Daily Telegram*, December 10, 1896.

50–51   Ibid.

54   Unidentified article in Taylor's personal scrapbook.

55–56 "Major Taylors Life in Danger," *Worcester Daily Telegram*, vol. XII, No. 107, 1, n.d.

58 Taylor, 30.

58–59 "Taylor Says It Is So," *Worcester Daily Telegram*, September 20, 1897, 4.

59 Bob Percival, "Remembering Father, the Bike Champ," The *Indianapolis Star Magazine*, February 12, 1984, 24.

62 "Out for a 1.10 Mile!" *Worcester Daily Telegram*, November 20, 1899, 1.

62–63 *Montreal Gazette*, August 11, 1899.

63 Ritchie, 125–126.

64 Taylor, 91: *Worcester Daily Telegram*, February 21, 1900.

65–66 Southwick, Albert, "Neighborhood Fought Sports Hero's Residency," *Telegram & Gazette*, January 21, 2000.

68 Unidentified article in Taylor's scrapbook.

69 Taylor, 104.

75 Ibid., 143.

81 Ibid., 159.

81 *Morning Herald* (Sydney), "Cycling To-night's Carnival 'Major' Taylor in a Lap Dash," January 7, 1903.

82 Ritchie, 202.

82–83 Taylor, 199.

83 Percival, 25.

86 *Chicago Daily Tribune*, May 17, "Taylor Last in Paris Race," 1909, 13.

86 Personal letters from Taylor to his wife from Taylor's scrapbook, 1910.

90 Percival, 24.

91 Ibid., 25.

91 Ritchie, 233–234.

91 Percival, 25.

92 Harry Worcester Smith, "A Champion Laid Low," *Worcester Evening Gazette*, December 17, 1926.

SELECTED BIBLIOGRAPHY

NEWSPAPERS AND MAGAZINES

Much of the information about Taylor's life and the times he lived in came from his autobiography, *The Fastest Bicycle Rider in the World*. But I found almost as many tidbits from articles written about him and letters he wrote to others. Taylor arranged many of these articles and letters to his wife in scrapbooks. His daughter, Sydney Taylor Brown, donated the scrapbooks to the Indiana State Museum, where I was able to read them.

Many scrapbook articles came from the *Worcester Daily Telegram, New York Times, Chicago Tribune, Boston Globe, Boston Post, Sydney Telegraph,* the *Daily Telegraph, Sydney Mail, Sydney Herald, Sportsman, Cycling, New York Herald, Indianapolis Sentinel, Indianapolis Press,* and the *Brooklyn Daily.* Several were unmarked, which makes exact documentation tricky. I also researched archives in Chicago, such as the *Chicago Defender*, Worcester (special folders in the library), and Indiana (special folders in the library) in addition to general bicycling journals, such as *The Wheel, Cycle Age, The Ledger* (special edition on bicycling), *Bicycling World,* and *Bearings.*

BOOKS

Alderson, Frederick. *Bicycling: A History.* New York: Praeger, 1972.

Baker, Ray. *Following the Color Line.* New York: Harper Torchbooks, 1964.

Bicycling Magazine editors. *Riding & Racing Techniques.* Emmaus, PA: Rodale Press, 1985.

Gibbs, Wilma, ed. *Indiana's African-American Heritage.* Indianapolis: Indiana Historical Society, 1993.

Leete, Harley, ed. *The Best of Bicycling!* New York: Trident Press, 1970.

McCullagh, James. *American Bicycle Racing.* Emmaus, PA: Rodale Press, 1976.

Nye, Peter. *Hearts of Lions: The History of American Bicycle Racing.* New York: W. W. Norton, 1988.

Pridmore, Jay, and Jim Hurd. *The American Bicycle.* Osceola, WI: Motorbooks, 1995.

Ritchie, Andrew. *King of the Road: An Illustrated History of Cycling.* Berkeley, CA: Ten Speed Press, 1975.

Smith, Robert. *The Social History of the Bicycle.* New York: American Heritage Press, 1972.

Taylor, Marshall Major. *The Fastest Bicycle Rider in the World.* Brattleboro, VT: Stephen Greene Press, 1928.

SPECIAL COLLECTIONS AND ORGANIZATIONS

The archives below maintain collections of various clippings, articles, advertisements, programs, and letters that pertain to Taylor's life and career.

Indiana Historical Society
450 West Ohio Street
Indianapolis, IN 46202-3269
http://www.indianahistory.org

Indiana State Library
140 North Senate Avenue
Indianapolis, IN 46204-2296
317-232-3675
http://www.statelib.lib.in.us

Indiana State Museum
202 North Alabama Street
Indianapolis, IN 46204
317-232-1637
http://www.indianamuseum.org
This museum has the largest collection of Taylor's memorabilia, including scrapbooks, letters, and awards.

Worcester Public Library
160 Fremont Street
Worcester, MA 01603-2362
508-799-1670
http://www.worcpublib.org

TO LEARN MORE ABOUT TAYLOR, BICYCLING, AND HIS TIMES

BOOKS

Collier, Christopher. *Reconstruction and the Rise of Jim Crow, 1864–1896*. White Plains, NY: Benchmark Books, 2000.

Greene, Meg. *Into the Land of Freedom*. Minneapolis: Twenty-First Century Books, 2004.

Haskins, Jim. *One More River to Cross: The Stories of Twelve Black Americans*. New York: Scholastic, 1992.

Kurtz, Jane, *Bicycle Madness*. New York: Henry Holt, 2002.

Scioscia, Mary. *Bicycle Rider*. New York: Harper & Row, 1983.

Wilds, Mary. *A Forgotten Champion*. Greensboro, NC: Avisson Press, 2002.

Wormser, Richard. *The Rise and Fall of Jim Crow.: The African-American Struggle Against Discrimination, 1865–1954*. New York: Franklin Watts, 1999.

WEBSITES

Freetown Village
http://www.Freetown.org
This site details lives of former slaves during the 1870s in the fourth ward in Indianapolis, where Taylor was born.

The History of Jim Crow
http://www.jimcrowhistory.org
The site features access to information, readings, television shows, and other material about African Americans from the Civil War through the 1950s.

League of American Bicyclists (formerly League of American Wheelmen)
http://www.bikeleague.org
Here is information about a leading cycling organization in the United States, its history, missions through the years, and current programs for bicyclists.

Major Taylor Association
http://www.majortaylorassociation.org
This site provides articles, school guides, additional resources, and other information about Major Taylor and how to learn more about him.
USA Cycling
http://usacycling.org
This site is for current bicycling enthusiasts who dream, like Taylor did, of reaching the top in racing.

VIDEO

Fitzpatrick, Jim, and Tony Morphatt. *Tracks of Glory*. VHS. Directed by Marcus Cole. [Australia TV], 1992.

PLACES TO VISIT

Bicycle Museum of America
7 West Monroe Street
New Bremen, OH 45869
419-629-9249
http://www.bicyclemuseum.com

Metz Bicycle Museum
54 West Main Street
Freehold, NJ 07728
732-462-7363
http://www.metzbicyclemuseum.com

INDEX

Jaquelin, Edmund, 74, 75
Jim Crow laws, 57
Johnson, Jack, 83, 84

Keith Vaudeville Company, 70
Kentucky, 9
Korbel Lifetime Achievement Award, 98–99

Lawson, Ivor, 82
League of American Wheelmen (LAW), 37, 40, 46, 67, 99
"Le Nègre Volant" (The Flying Black Man), 84

MacFarland, Floyd, 78, 79, 82
Madison Square Garden, 49; six-day race in, 48–51
Major Taylor Association, 97
Major Taylor Bike Trail, 97–98
Major Taylor Manufacturing Company, 90
Major Taylor: The Extraordinary Career of a Champion Bicycle Racer, 98
Major Taylor Velodrome, 97, 99
manager, 53
McLeod, Angus, 62
Metcalf, Ralph, 95
Morris, Daisy. *See* Taylor, Daisy Morris (wife)
Munger, Louis "Birdie," 31–32, 33, 34, 41, 46
Munger Cycle Manufacturing Company, 32

National Circuit Riders (NCR), 58, 67, 68, 77, 83; bans Taylor, 67
Newby Oval track, 69

Olde Tymers Athletic Club, 94–95

Parker, C. A., 15

Philadelphia Centennial Exposition, 15
Plessy v. Ferguson, 57
Pope, Albert, 15
Poulain, Gabriel, 86
prices, 59
prize money, 74

racism, 7, 8–9, 13, 16, 37, 41, 57, 82; in bicycle racing, 29, 30, 37, 54–56, 78, 99; in education, 19; in housing, 65; lack of in Europe, 71, 74, 77, 78. *See also* Taylor, Marshall Walter "Major": racism
Rice, Daddy, 57
riding lessons, bicycle, 28–29
Ritchie, Andrew, 98
Robinson, Jackie, 7

Sager, Harry, 61
Sager Gear Company, 61
Sanger, Walter, 29–30
Schwinn, Frank, 94–95
Schwinn Bicycle Company, 95
scratch man, 25
segregation, 57
six-day bicycle race, 7, 48–51
slavery, 8, 9, 13
Smith, Harry Worcester, 91–92
South, racism in, 54, 57
Southard, Daniel, 10, 18
Southard family, 10, 13, 18; Taylor's life with, 10–13, 16, 18
speed records, 30, 61, 65
sports, 6, 7, 16, 84; children's, 11–12
Springfield, IL, 26
Starley, James, 14
Supreme Court, rules on racism, 57

Taylor, Daisy Morris (wife), 71–72, 78, 79, 80, 81, 84, 86, 89, 91, 92
Taylor, Gertrude (sister), 10, 65, 67, 68
Taylor, Gilbert (father), 8, 9, 69

110

Taylor, Louis, 72, 78

Taylor, Marshall Walter "Major": achievements of, 6–7, 59–63, 65, 70, 79; attacks, on, 46–47, 55, 83; Australia tour, 79–82, 98; autobiography of, 91, 92, 93, 94; banned from racing, 30, 35, 67, 98; birth and early childhood, 8–13, 16–17; businesses, 90; buys house, 65–66; death of, 94–95; diary, 59, 71; earnings, 50, 53, 62, 74, 79, 89; education, 11, 13, 19, 90; European tours, 71, 72–77, 78, 85–87; farm life, 18–19; fatherhood, 81, 83; first race, 23–25; goals, 59, 68; health, 90, 94; inventor, 89–90; jobs, 10, 19, 21, 26, 27, 32, 44, 89, 93, 94; lawsuits against, 83; life with Southards, 10–13,16, 18; marriage, 71–72, 78, 92–93; money troubles, 90–92, 94; nervous breakdown, 83; nicknames, 22, 47, 68, 84; no-Sunday-racing rule, 59, 67, 71, 79, 83–84, 85; personality, 7, 24, 58–59, 64, 66, 78, 92; popularity of, 54, 73, 77, 80–81, 84, 92; professional racer, 48, 51; racism and, 7, 16–17, 46, 54–56, 58, 65, 78, 82–83, 84, 91; religion, 19, 59, 78, 83; retires, 87; sets records, 30, 53–54, 60–61, 65, 86; training, 34, 44–45, 85, 90; trick rider, 20, 21, 29, 44, 47, 70; in vaudeville, 70

Taylor, Rita Sydney (daughter). *See* Brown, Sydney Taylor

Taylor, Saphronia, 8, 9, 10, 18, 22, 25, 27, 37; death of, 59

tires, air-filled, 26–27

tracks, bicycle racing, 35, 49, 68–69, 97

Tracks of Glory, 98

trading cards, 6, 76

trick riding, 20

Twain, Mark, 15

vaudeville, 70

velodromes, 35, 97

Walker, Benjamin, 45

Washington, Booker T., 82–83

Windle, Willie, 33, 34

women, 38, 43; bicycles and, 38–39

Worcester, MA, 41, 43, 44, 97

Worcester Cycle Manufacturing Company, 43–44

work and workers, 9, 13, 19, 53

World Championship (bicycle racing), 62–63

YMCA, 16, 44, 45, 93–94

Zig-Zag Club, 29, 37

Zimmerman, Arthur, 32–33, 68, 79

ABOUT THE AUTHOR

Marlene Targ Brill is an award-winning author of more than sixty-five books. She often writes about young people and how they overcome great odds to follow their dreams. Major Taylor is one of those people from history. Marlene likes that she lives near Chicago, Illinois, where Major rests in peace with honor.

PHOTO ACKNOWLEDGMENTS

The images in this book are used with the permission of: The collection of the Indiana State Museum and Historic Sites, pp. 2, 8, 18, 26, 36, 42, 43, 52, 53, 60, 61, 64, 72, 73, 77, 80, 81, 88, 89, 97; Library of Congress, pp. 9 (LC-US262-97708), 40 (rbpe 20702200), 44 (pan 6a05944), 45 (pan 6a06129), 49 (LC-DIG-ggbain-01531), 79 (LC-DIG-ggbain-03005), 84 (LC-USZ62-29331), 87 (LC-DIG-ggbain-03006); The Art Archive/Culver Pictures, p. 11; © Hulton Archive/ Getty Images, pp. 12, 27, 38; The Art Archive/Musée National de la voiture et du tourisme Compiégne/Dagli Orti, p. 14; Culver Pictures, pp. 20, 34; © Bass Photo Co. Collection/Indiana Historical Society, p. 28; National Museum of American History, Smithsonian Institute, p. 31; © Brown Brothers, p. 39; Courtesy of the Ohio Historical Society, p. 55; Schomburg Center for Research in Black Culture, Photographs and Prints Division, p. 56; Courtesy of Marlene Targ Brill, p. 66; © Bettmann/CORBIS, p. 71; © Getty Images, p, 76; Courtesy of the City of Chicago, Commission on Chicago Landmarks., p. 93; Courtesy of Kautz Family YMCA Archives. University of Minnesota Libraries, p. 94; © Boyer/Roger-Viollet/The Image Works, p. 85; Courtesy of Calvin Spencer/The Home Depot Center/U.S. Bicycle Hall of Fame, p. 98

Cover: Courtesy of the collection of the Indiana State Museum and Historic Sites